Sea View Camping

SCOTLAND, HIGHLANDS AND ISLANDS

Vicarious Media

Derived from a guide first published in Great Britain by Brian M. Leahy, 2006. Reprinted 2007.
Republished 2008 and 2010 by Vicarious Books Ltd.
This variant published 2014. Reprinted by Vicarious Media 2015.

Vicarious Media, 62 Tontine Street, Folkestone, Kent, CT20 1JP. Tel: 0131 2083333

Editors: Chris Doree, Pami Hoggatt, Caroline Stacey and Meli George

Design and artwork by: Chris Gladman Design Tel: 07745 856652

Front cover
Main picture: Eilean Donan Castle, © www.BritainOnView.com.
Small pictures: Queensberry Bay, Glenbrittle and North Ledaig.

Back cover
Small pictures: Uig Bay and Kinloch.

What's inside this unique guide?

This unique guide shows and tells you about the sea view campsites around Scotland, the Highlands and Islands. There are campsites perched on the edge of craggy cliff tops, and plenty alongside deserted sandy beaches lapped by crystal clear sea loch waters. With sites ranging from the largest holiday parks near major towns like Edinburgh to small, community-run sites less than 200 miles from the coast of Norway, all you have to do is decide upon where you want to go and be ready for a fantastic time as you explore the lochs, forests, moors and mountains.

Barry Crawshaw embarked on a series of inspection tours searching out potential sea view campsites along the way. His brief was to include every campsite with a sea view, and as far as is possible that has been done. The result is that you are now reading the most comprehensive compilation of sea view campsites located around the Scottish mainland, the Inner and Outer Hebrides including the Isles of Skye and Mull, and the Orkney and Shetland Islands.

To help you make informed choices, each listing includes a photo and a description of the sea view. The quality of the facilities and amenities are not formally judged, but are listed and commented upon. Where appropriate the local area and attractions are mentioned. Beach access is normally easy, but this is discussed as necessary. In addition, the location of the nearest pub, shop, beach and slipway is provided to further assist you.

When available the campsite's own website address is provided. Should any updates or amendments be made known to us, these will be published at http://www.vicariousbooks.co.uk/guide_updates.shtml

Oban

HOW TO USE THIS GUIDE

Campsite location – The numbers printed on the map on page 15 identify and locate each campsite. The campsites are listed geographically and in map number order on pages 8-9. Use this list to find the map reference number, the campsite name and the page number of the listing. Page numbers can also be found by campsite name using the alphabetical index at the rear.

Entry explanation

1 **Campsite name**

2 **Campsite map reference number**

3 **Campsite address and phone number**

4 **Campsite website, where available**

5 **Photo of the sea view from the campsite**

6 **Units accepted by campsite**

   Å   *Tent*

   🚐   *Touring caravan*

   🚐   *Motorhome*

   🚌 *Large vehicles* - Motorhomes/Caravans/5th Wheels. Campsites were checked for accessibility and the owners/managers were asked whether large vehicles were accommodated on the site. Where highlighted, access should be possible for competent and experienced drivers. Most campsites only accept very large vehicles with advanced bookings and we insist that you discuss access and pitch availability with campsite staff before arrival.

   🚐 *Holiday accommodation for hire* – Many of the campsites in this guide have other accommodation for hire (i.e. static caravans, holiday homes, chalets, or lodges). This accommodation has not been inspected and may not have the sea view described in the listing.

7 **Description** – An unbiased description is given of the site and the sea view. The strengths or weaknesses and appeal of the site are provided. Further useful information is also given.

8 **Symbols** – The following symbols are used to identify the size and facilities of the site. All sites have a water tap and a toilet disposal point unless otherwise stated. Facility only available when highlighted.

  NA Number of acres where known
  NP Number of pitches
  🔌 Electricity available and amperage where known
  ⚡ Level pitches
  ⚡ All season/hardstanding pitches
  WC Toilets
  ♿ Disabled toilets

  🝊 Showers
  🛁 Family bathroom/shower room
  🝑 Dishwashing facilities
  🔲 Laundry
  MG Motorhome wastewater disposal
  MB Motorhome toilet waste disposal

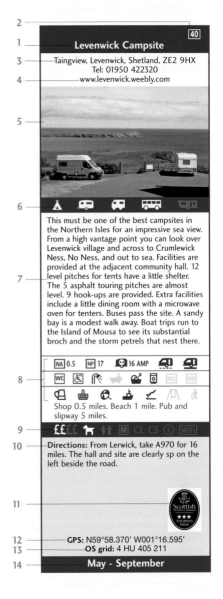

1 **Levenwick Campsite**   40

3 Taingview, Levenwick, Shetland, ZE2 9HX
Tel: 01950 422320
4 www.levenwick.weebly.com

6 Å 🚐 🚐 🚌 🚐

7 This must be one of the best campsites in the Northern Isles for an impressive sea view. From a high vantage point you can look over Levenwick village and across to Crumlewick Ness, No Ness, and out to sea. Facilities are provided at the adjacent community hall. 12 level pitches for tents have a little shelter. The 5 asphalt touring pitches are almost level. 9 hook-ups are provided. Extra facilities include a little dining room with a microwave oven for tenters. Buses pass the site. A sandy bay is a modest walk away. Boat trips run to the Island of Mousa to see its substantial broch and the storm petrels that nest there.

8 NA 0.5 NP 17 🔌 16 AMP ⚡ ⚡
  WC ♿ 🝊 🛁 🝑 🔲 MG MB
  🔲 🝑 🔍 🛁 ✂ ⛰ 🧍
Shop 0.5 miles. Beach 1 mile. Pub and slipway 5 miles.

9 ££££ 🐕 👫 M CL CS ⓘ WiFi

10 **Directions:** From Lerwick, take A970 for 16 miles. The hall and site are clearly sp on the left beside the road.

12 **GPS:** N59°58.370' W001°16.595'
13 **OS grid:** 4 HU 405 211
14 **May - September**

The following symbols identify amenities that are either onsite or within five minutes walk, unless otherwise indicated. The facilities have not been tested and charges may apply.

🍺 Pub/bar
🏪 Shop
🏖 Beach
⚓ Slipway
🏊 Indoor or Outdoor swimming pool
🛝 Children's play area
🚶 Footpath

9 **Information Symbols**

Cost – The cost of the campsite is indicated by the £ symbols. All prices are based on two people in one caravan or motorhome with electric during August. Prices are offered as a guideline only and should always be confirmed in advance.

£ Up to £10 per night
££ £10-17 per night
£££ £17-35 per night
££££ £35 or more per night

🐕 Many campsites allow dogs onsite, indicated by the dog symbol, but confirmation must always be sought in advance that your dog(s) can be accommodated. Many campsites charge extra for dogs, there may be a limit on the number of dogs allowed onsite, and some sites specify the type of units that dogs can be accommodated in. Some sites also have breed restrictions, so always check your breed is permitted before arrival. Campsite owners and other holidaymakers expect dogs to be kept quiet and under control, and usually on a lead, at all times. Dogs must be exercised in appropriate areas, or offsite, and all mess must be cleared in a responsible fashion. In addition, it is advised that you never leave your dog unattended.

👫 This symbol refers to adult only campsites. No person under the age of 18 will be admitted.

Ⓜ This symbol refers to member only campsites. Generally these belong to either the Camping and Caravanning Club or the Caravan Club and a valid membership is required to stay, though it may be possible to join at reception. The name of the club is usually indicated in the title of the campsite. CS and CL sites are also for members only.

CS *(Certified Sites)* - These sites are for Camping and Caravanning Club members only. These are small sites, restricted to five caravans or motorhomes, plus tents space permitting.

CL *(Certified Locations)* - These sites are for Caravan Club members only. These are small sites, restricted to five caravans or motorhomes.

ⓘ Internet available (charges may apply).

WiFi WiFi available (charges may apply).

10 **Directions** – Directions are provided. Please note that many campsites near the sea are down narrow lanes with passing places.

11 **Awards** – Scottish tourist board awarded star ratings.

12 **GPS Coordinates** – Coordinates are presented in true GPS format. Our office, for example, is located at N51° 04.895' E001° 10.978'. You may need to select this format in your navigator's menu. Coordinates were recorded at the site entrance, or sometimes the approach road/driveway, to prevent navigator error. We have provided directions that should be suitable for most vehicles but your navigator may not, so ensure that you check the route against a map and our directions. Please note that postcodes often do not provide accurate destinations when used with satellite navigators.

13 **OS grid references** – The six figure grid references provided refer to locations on the Ordinance Survey Landranger 1:50,000 sheet map series. The first three numbers and the two letters refer to the map identification code. The remaining numbers create a six-digit grid reference. Unlike the GPS coordinates, these will locate the campsite rather than the entrance.

14 **Opening dates** – Opening dates change year to year and are given as an indication only, please check with the campsite before arrival.

15 **Advanced booking** – You will need to contact the individual campsites to make advanced bookings, especially if you are planning a visiting during the summer holidays or other peak periods.

Abbreviations
mins = minutes   sp = signposted

Vicarious Shop

- MMM Essential, '...pleasurable reading for novice or old hand'. *Barry Crawshaw.*
- Practical Motorhome '...it's jam-packed with information on touring...' *Sarah Wakely.*
- Motor caravanner 'It really is a powerhouse of information plus hints and tips based on real active motorcaravanners' experiences both at home and abroad.' *Gentleman Jack.*

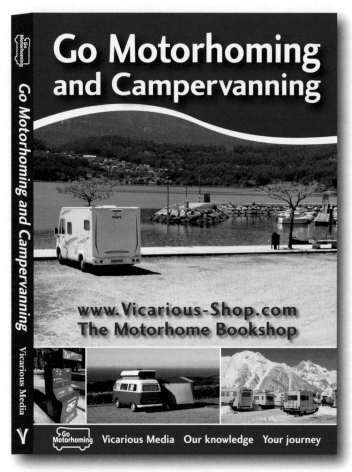

Motorhoming and Campervanning is a complicated subject so chapter by chapter your knowledge will build, and everything you need to know is fully explained, not just how things work but also what that means to you. Real life examples clarify the point and colour pictures show you exactly what to look for. From planning your first trip abroad, a winter sun escape or a long term tour, Go Motorhoming covers it all.

To order, give us a call or visit our website to buy online.

Tel: 0131 2083333 www.Vicarious-Shop.com

Award collection, Argyll Holiday Park

Restored black houses are popular holiday lets

CONTENTS

CONTENTS

Vicarious Shop

Don't get lost, get your maps from www.Vicarious-Shop.com. Extensive range of road atlases and sheet maps for the UK and Europe all sold at RRP with free UK P&P.

To order, give us a call or visit our website to buy online.

Tel: 0131 2083333 www.Vicarious-Shop.com

Essence of the north west coast

Meeting the locals

Vicarious Shop

Motorhomers and campervanners have the privilege of stopping overnight all over Europe at stopovers known as Aires. For more information, visit www.all-the-aires.co.uk.

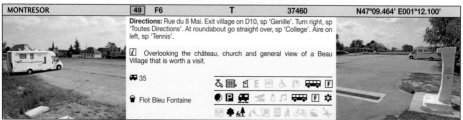

| MONTRESOR | 49 | F6 | T | 37460 | N47°09.464' E001°12.100' |

Directions: Rue du 8 Mai. Exit village on D10, sp 'Genille'. Turn right, sp 'Toutes Directions'. At roundabout go straight over, sp 'College'. Aire on left, sp 'Tennis'.

Overlooking the château, church and general view of a Beau Village that is worth a visit.

35

Flot Bleu Fontaine

Sample France entry with corresponding mapping. Similar mapping for Spain and Portugal and Belgium, Luxembourg and Holland.

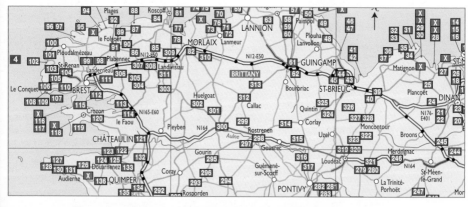

To order, give us a call or visit our website to buy online.

Tel: 0131 2083333   www.Vicarious-Shop.com

Vicarious Shop

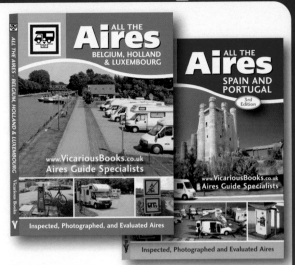

- 2700 Aires for France
- 303 Aires for Spain and Portugal
- 121 Aires for Holland
- 78 Aires for Belgium, plus 10 for Luxembourg
- Extensive LPG listings for every country

Sample Spain and Portugal entry. Entries for Belgium, Luxembourg and Holland follow the same format.

| BOIRO ★ | ⚓ B2 | 64 | N42°38.503' W008°53.816' | 15930 |

Directions: Avenida Compostela. From AC305, main route through Boiro, turn off when signed - signed from both directions. Road has 3.5t weight restriction. Follow road down to sea. Designated parking in car park opp beach.

Sanitation:

Parking:

🚐 8; €6 May-Oct; €3 Nov-Apr; Max 72hrs; Parking ticket purchased from police station in town

Custom; WC emptying by road

ℹ This is a popular beachside Aire with good views of the crystal clear sea. The golden sandy beach is just across the coast road. There are rocks to snorkel amongst and small fishing boats to watch. Behind the Aire there is a children's play area and green space with BBQs amongst trees. There is a pleasant bar adj and town commerce is 5 mins.

Leisure Information:

Lifeline of the Western Isles

Strangest toilet building on Shetland

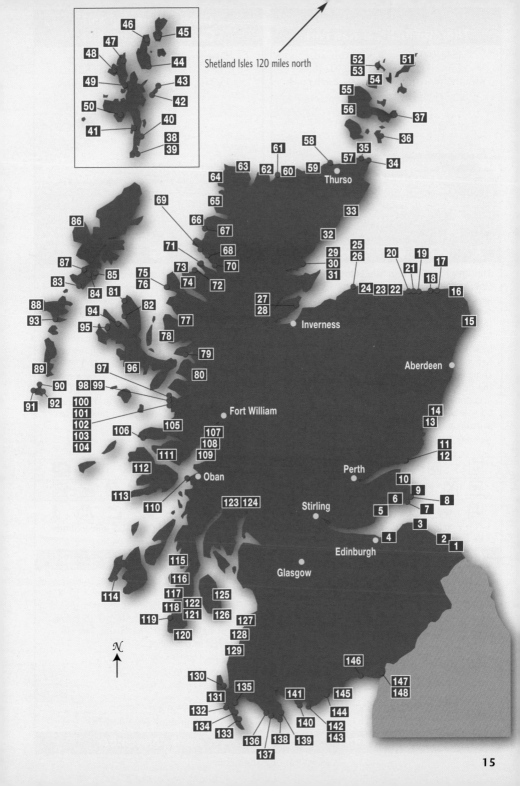

Shetland Isles 120 miles north

Thurso

Inverness

Aberdeen

Fort William

Oban

Perth

Stirling

Edinburgh

Glasgow

N

15

Thorntonloch Caravan Park [1]

Innerwick, Dunbar, East Lothian,
EH42 1QS Tel: 01368 840236
www.thorntonlochcaravanpark.vpweb.co.uk

This immaculately kept site is located alongside its own beautiful sandy surfing beach interspersed with rock pools. Statics occupy most of the site. Of the scattered touring pitches, all with electricity, 8 on hardstanding in the front row look over the beach and across the sea to St Abbs Head. Remaining from a centuries-old fishing community, beautiful stone buildings include the original smoke-house, and 2 of them accommodate washrooms that were completely refurbished for 2013. Surfers provide a spectacle for campers. John Muir walkway passes the site.

| NA | 1.5 | NP | 10 | 10 AMP | | |

| WC | | | | | | MG | MB |

Pub 7 miles. Shop 3 miles. Small boats can be launched from beach. Slipway 2 miles.

£££ CL CS WiFi

Directions: 7 miles south of Dunbar on A1, turn towards the sea sp 'Thorntonloch'. Follow the lane for 0.25 miles to the site.

GPS: N55°57.778' W002°23.988'
OS grid: 67 NT 751 745

March - October

Dunbar Camping and Caravanning Club Site [2]

Oxwellmains, Dunbar, East Lothian,
EH42 1WG Tel: 01368 866881
www.campingandcaravanningclub.co.uk

This purpose-built site was opened in September 2008 with all new facilities and amenities. All pitches have electricity and can accept units up to 10m/32ft. Most give a view past May Island and Bass Rock to the Fife coast. Gannets scour the sea just off the sandy beach, which is about an 8 mins walk away. A cycle path leads to an Asda 1 mile away. Dunbar, about 7 miles away by a quiet, cyclable road, has a fine swimming pool, adventure playground, slipway and several places to eat out. A geological trail is also located nearby.

| NA | | NP | 90 | 16 AMP | | |

| WC | | | | | | MG | MB |

Shops, pubs and slipway 2.5 miles. Sandy beach 0.25 miles.

£££ CL CS WiFi

Directions: Do not drive through Dunbar. From A1 southeast of Dunbar, take A1087 sp 'Dunbar'. After 0.25 miles, go straight ahead at the roundabout. After 0.25 miles, turn 1st right sp to the campsite. The site is on the left in 0.5 miles.

GPS: N55°59.470' W002°28.812'
OS grid: 67 NT 700 778

April - November

Tantallon Caravan and Camping Park

North Berwick, East Lothian, EH39 5NJ
Tel: 01620 893348
www.meadowhead.co.uk

Overlooking the Firth of Forth from an elevated position, this is truly a magnificent spot. All the pitches provide a glorious view of the Bass Rock and the fascinating small islands. Static caravans occupy one side of the site and tourers the other. Most of the pitches have electricity, are on grass, and slope very slightly. About 25 are on level hardstanding. Motorhomes of any length can be accommodated. The Glen Golf Course spreads out in front of the campsite and a footpath takes you 0.25 miles across the golf course to the sandy beach.

NA	10	NP	140	10 AMP		
WC					MG	MB

Pub 750m. Tesco 5 mins walk. Slipway in North Berwick. Pool 1.5 miles.

£££ 🐕 †† M CL CS ⓘ WiFi

Directions: Eastbound on A1 at Haddington roundabout, turn onto A199 sp 'East Linton', then 'Dunbar'. After 6 miles, turn left onto A198 sp 'North Berwick'. The site is on the right after 7 miles.

GPS: N56°03.338' W002°41.433'
OS grid: 67 NT 570 850

March - October

Seton Sands Holiday Village

Links Road, Port Seton, East Lothian,
EH32 0QF Tel: 01875 813333
www.haven.com

This very large holiday park lies east of Edinburgh. In the tourers area, a hedge with gaps allows a few pitches to have a distant view of the Forth Estuary. The beach of sand and rock stretches to extensive sand flats at low water. The all-grass pitches have electricity and are soft when wet. Some are reinforced by strong plastic mesh. Typical for a big resort, the facilities include entertainment, a sports hall, orienteering, a chip shop and Spar provisions shop. Buses from the park entrance run to Edinburgh every 20 mins.

NA	1.5	NP	34	10 AMP		
WC					MG	MB

Slipway 1 mile.

££££ 🐕 †† M CL CS ⓘ WiFi

Directions: On A1 westbound from Dunbar, continue past Haddington for 5 miles. At a roundabout, turn right onto B6363. Pass under a railway bridge and turn right onto A198 for 2 miles. At the sea, turn left onto B1348 for 1.5 miles to the site on the left.

GPS: N55°58.342' W002°55.850'
OS grid: 66 NT 422 758

March - October

Leven Beach Holiday Park

North Promenade, Leven, Fife, KY8 4HY
Tel: 01333 426008
www.pettycur.co.uk/levenbeach.asp

Beyond the statics lies a compact touring area. From the front row of pitches beside the boundary fence, the view is past the sandy beach and across the wide Firth of Forth towards North Berwick. The level grass pitches all have electricity. At the main building are a bar, shop, and amusements. A golf course borders the site and the Fife Coastal Path passes by. The town and the seaside's entertainment and bucket-and-spade shops are within walking distance.

| NA | 0.5 | NP | 20 | 16 AMP | | |

| WC | | | | | | MG | MB |

Slipway 3 miles.

£££ £ †† M CL CS (i) WiFi

Directions: From north or west, follow A955 to the roundabout on Leven seafront. From there, follow the seafront northeastwards to the site.

GPS: N56°12.048' W002°58.993'
OS grid: 59 NO 391 014

March - October

Monturpie Caravan Park

Upper Largo, Near St Andrews,
Fife, KY8 5QS
Tel: 01333 360254 www.monturpie.co.uk

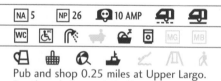

On a hill, Monturpie Guest House and Restaurant is a traditional, stone-built farmhouse. Both the campsite and restaurant have fantastic views overlooking the Firth of Forth towards Edinburgh and Leith. This adult-only site is beautifully cared for, with luxurious, recently built toilets and showers. All the spacious pitches have electricity, most are level, and 17 are hard. Monturpie also has a CL. The coffee shop and renowned, licensed restaurant are open Wednesday to Sunday. A 15 mins walk downhill takes you to a wonderful little village shop.

| NA | 5 | NP | 26 | 10 AMP | | |

| WC | | | | | | MG | MB |

Pub and shop 0.25 miles at Upper Largo. Beach and slipway 1.5 miles.

£££ £ †† M CL CS (i) WiFi

Directions: Located halfway between Kirkcaldy and St Andrews adjacent to A915, 0.5 miles north of Upper Largo village.

GPS: N56°13.465' W002°54.954'
OS grid: 59 NO 434 038

March - October

Elie Holiday Park

Shell Bay, Elie, Fife, KY9 1HB
Tel: 01333 330283
www.abbeyford.com/our-parks

Photo courtesy of owner

From a low bank beside the sandy beach, the touring area rises gradually, giving most pitches some outlook up the Forth Estuary. On slightly undulating turf over hard sand, all pitches have electricity, most are level and some partly gravelled. Onsite are an adventure playground, floral displays, a restaurant and take-away. The adjacent pine forest is popular for walking, running and cycling. Fife Coastal Path passes the site. Close by are historic Earlsferry and Elie with a golf course and a sheltered bay that buzzes with various water sports.

NA	5	NP	120	10 AMP		

Slipway 3 miles.

££££ 🐕 †† M CL CS (i) WiFi

Directions: 1.5 miles northwest of Elie, turn off A917 onto a well sp, single-track road with passing places. Follow this through the forest for 1.25 miles to the site.

GPS: N56°11.631' W002°51.400'
OS grid: 59 NO 464 004

March - October

Silverdyke Caravan Park

Windmill Road, Cellardyke, Anstruther, Fife, KY10 3FN Tel: 01333 313098
www.silverdykepark.co.uk

Atop a 20m cliff, half the pitches have a clear view across the lower Forth Estuary past the Isle of May to the East Lothian coast. A thin hedge breaks up the view from others. Local fishing boats pass to and fro, and large vessels are seen further off. Newly constructed in 2012, all pitches are level, hard, and fully serviced. Facilities are to the highest standard and include a games room. In Anstruther are the outstanding Scottish Fisheries Museum and a renowned fish restaurant. Charming East Neuk fishing villages of Crail, Pittenweem and St Monans are a few miles away.

NA	16	NP	30	16 AMP		

Shop and slipway 0.5 miles.

££££ 🐕 †† M CL CS (i) WiFi

Directions: From St Andrews on A917, pass through Crail towards Anstruther. Immediately after passing the hamlet of Kilrenny, turn left at the outskirts of Anstruther into Windmill Road. At a mini-roundabout, turn at the site sign into the site driveway, towards the conspicuous war memorial on the clifftop. Owner recommends using KY10 3EN when inputting address into your satnav.

GPS: N56°13.695' W002°41.223'
OS grid: 59 NO 577 043

March - November

Sauchope Links Caravan Park 〔9〕

The Links, Crail, Fife, KY10 3XJ
Tel: 01333 450460
www.largoleisure.co.uk

Beautifully maintained with impeccable facilities, the site is mostly level although parts are sloping. Near the rocky shore are 50 touring pitches of which 20 are on level hardstanding. All the front row pitches have a wide, uninterrupted view across the outer Forth Estuary to May Island and the East Lothian coast. Tent pitches are limited to 2. Drivers of motorhomes over 8m long should enquire in advance. Within walking distance is the charming town of Crail, with its steep, narrow streets, harbour and sandy beach. Fife Coastal Path passes through the site.

| NA 20 | NP 50 | ☠ 16 AMP | | |

| WC | 🖐 | 🚿 | 🛁 | 🍴 | ▢ | MG | MB |

Shop and pub 0.5 miles.

£££ £ 🐕 †† Ⓜ CL CS ⓘ WiFi

Directions: From St Andrews or the southeast coast of Fife, take A917 to Crail. From the roundabout at the right-angle bend in the road, continue northeastwards for nearly 0.5 miles. After the last houses on the right, turn right along a narrow road to the site.

GPS: N56°15.697' W002°36.783'
OS grid: 59 NO 623 079

mid March - October

St Andrews Holiday Park 〔10〕

Kinkell Braes, St Andrews, Fife, KY16 8PX
Tel: 01334 474250
www.abbeyford.com/our-parks

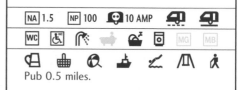

From each of two areas for tourers, some pitches give views interrupted by statics and trees. The panorama from this large, elevated site is truly spectacular, taking in the East Sands, harbour, and West Sands where sand yachts sometimes dash about. Beyond are Tentsmuir Forest, the Tay Estuary, and the coast and distant hills of Angus. All touring pitches have electricity, most are on grass, and 6 are level. A bar, restaurant, entertainment, shop, and games room are all on site.

| NA 1.5 | NP 100 | ☠ 10 AMP | | |

| WC | 🖐 | 🚿 | 🛁 | 🍴 | ▢ | MG | MB |

Pub 0.5 miles.

£££ £ 🐕 †† Ⓜ CL CS ⓘ WiFi

Directions: From St Andrews, take A917 towards Crail. 0.25 miles after leaving the 30mph zone, turn left into the site.

GPS: N56°19.740' W002°46.462'
OS grid: 59 NO 525 156

March - October

Marine Drive, Monifieth, Angus,
DD5 4NN Tel: 01382 535471
www.riverview.co.uk

Of the mostly sheltered, hardstanding pitches on this well-maintained site, all have electricity. About 12 have a good view across the Tay Estuary whereas others have only a glimpse. Facilities that include a sauna, gym and games room are well painted and impeccably clean. Just beyond the boundary fence and hedge, the sandy beach is vast at low tide. Buses serve Dundee's attractions, and a path and NCN route 1 cycleway pass the site.

| NA | 5.5 | NP | 42 | ☠ 16 AMP | | |

| WC | ♿ | ⛿ | 🛁 | | ▣ | MG | MB |

| | | | | | | |

Pub and shop 5 mins walk.

£££**£** 🐕 ⅲ M CL CS ⓘ WiFi

Directions: From Dundee on A930, in Monifieth take the 1st right-hand turn past Tesco into Reform Street. At the end of the road turn left, then take the next road on the right under the bridge (height 3.2m; 10ft 6in). The site is sp on the left in 100m.

GPS: N56°28.766' W002°48.733'
OS grid: 54 NO 501 322

March - January

Marine Drive, Monifieth, Dundee,
DD5 4NL Tel: 01382 532837
www.tayview.info

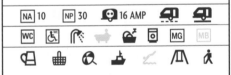

The level, mainly grass touring area offers 14 front row pitches with panoramic views over the Tay Estuary to Tentsmuir Forest. This increasingly popular site lies next to a beach of sand and rock, exploited at low tide by wading birds and bait diggers. Most of the touring pitches have electricity, and a fridge-freezer is available for campers. Security fencing separates the site from a waterfront footpath and cycleway, and screening hides the adjacent railway. The café on site serves full meals. Buses from nearby Monifieth High Street to Dundee take 30 mins.

| NA | 10 | NP | 30 | ☠ 16 AMP | | |

| WC | ♿ | ⛿ | 🛁 | | ▣ | MG | MB |

| | | | | | | |

£££**£** 🐕 ⅲ M CL CS ⓘ WiFi

Directions: Exit A92 halfway between Dundee and Arbroath onto B962 south. At the roundabout, take the 2nd exit. In the centre of Monifieth, turn left into Tay Street. After 250m, bend right, then turn left under the railway bridge (height 3.2m/10ft 6in). Turn right at the seafront, then 1st right. Take the 2nd left at the sign into the site. Owner recommends using DD5 4GH if inputting address into satnav, but use satnav with caution.

GPS: N56°28.783' W002°49.050'
OS grid: 54 NO 496 322

February - November

Miltonhaven Seaside Caravan Park |13|

St Cyrus, by Montrose, Kincardineshire,
DD10 0DL Tel: 01674 850413
www.miltonhaven.co.uk

The touring pitches include 4 for motorhomes directly beside a stony beach with unobstructed views of the open sea. Other pitches, also with sea views, are in a nearby paddock and 6 hardstandings are elsewhere. All have electricity. Book ahead for large motorhomes. Feel free to bring your own drinks to the characterful lounge which has a television, books and local information. Adjacent to the lounge is a kitchen and cosy little dining room for campers. The site has its own sandy swimming beach with rock pools nearby.

| NA 6 | NP 15 | 16 AMP | | |
| WC | | | | MG | MB |

Dogs allowed but not with tenters. Pub and shop 2 miles. Slipway 3.5 miles in Johnshaven.

£££ M CL CS WiFi

Directions: At the crossroads 2 miles north of St Cyrus on A92, turn southeast on B9120 towards the sea. The site is on the right in about 0.5 miles.

GPS: N56°46.830' W002°22.377'
OS grid: 45 NO 775 655

April - October

Wairds Park Caravan Site |14|

Beach Road, Johnshaven, Montrose,
Angus, DD10 0EP
Tel: 01561 362395

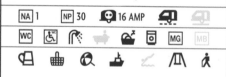

Benefitting from slightly rising ground, tourers have views between front row statics over a low wall and past the shore of pebbles and rock out over the North Sea. Managed by the enterprising community, the site offers 15 tent pitches, 2 with electricity, and 15 caravan pitches with electricity, all on virtually level, firm grass. Users of large motorhomes should phone to check availability of space. On site are a meeting room, putting, bowls, tennis, football and a splendid playground. Once one of Scotland's principal fishing ports, the harbour is still thronged with small inshore boats. A leaflet guides visitors on a historical stroll. Buses run from the square.

| NA 1 | NP 30 | 16 AMP | | |
| WC | | | | MG | MB |

££££ M CL CS WiFi

Directions: Northbound on A92, 9 miles north of Montrose, take the 1st turning sp 'Johnshaven'. Ignore all turnings before reaching the harbour. Turn left along Fore Street. Turn right at the T-junction onto Beach Road to the site.

GPS: N56°47.800' W002°19.600'
OS grid: 45 NO 803 674

April - October

Lido Caravan Park

South Road, Peterhead, Aberdeenshire,
AB42 2XX Tel: 01779 473358
www.aberdeenshire.gov.uk/caravanparks

There is plenty here to catch your attention as you look across the Peterhead Harbour of Refuge to the entrance, deep water trawlers and diverse oil-related vessels. Nearer at hand are the marina, yacht club and a wide sandy beach that begins close to the site. Enclosed by the breakwaters, the bay is popular for sailing and windsurfing. Benches and picnic tables are dotted along the beach edge. The former Aberdeenshire council site is now in the capable hands of Peterhead Projects, a community charitable trust. A short hose will be required when emptying motorhome wastewater tanks.

| NA 4 | NP 26 | 10 AMP | | |

Slipway adjacent.

£££

Directions: From the south, follow A90 to the outskirts of Peterhead. At the roundabout where A90 turns left, go straight ahead onto A982 South Road for 0.75 miles. Turn right, down into the site, sp 'Lido'.

GPS: N57°29.805' W001°47.740'
OS grid: 30 NK 124 452

March - October

Esplanade Caravan Park

The Esplanade, Fraserburgh, Aberdeenshire,
AB43 9EU Tel: 01346 510041
www.aberdeenshire.gov.uk/caravanparks/locations/fraserburgh.asp

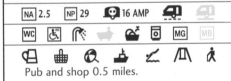

At one end of a mile-long arc of flat, sandy beach backed by dunes, the site looks across the sea to Cairnbulg Point at the northeast tip of Buchan. Surfers ride the breaking waves and kite buggies swish across the sand at low tide. All the level, well-drained grass pitches for tourers have electricity. Tents have plenty of additional space. Campers have easy access to the beach. Shops and attractions such as the Lighthouse and Heritage Museums are within walking distance.

| NA 2.5 | NP 29 | 16 AMP | | |

Pub and shop 0.5 miles.

££££

Directions: From south, take A90 just into Fraserburgh. At roundabout turn right onto B9033 South Harbour Road for approximately 0.75 miles. Turn right into the site sp 'Esplanade' with the campsite symbol.

GPS: N57°41.202' W002°00.079'
OS grid: 30 NK 000 663

April - October

Wester Bonnyton Caravan and Camping Site 〔17〕

Gamrie, Banff, AB45 3EP
Tel: 01261 832470
www.westerbonnyton.co.uk

Photo courtesy of Clare Doyle

Set on a hillside 0.5 miles back from the coast at an altitude of 100m, the site is steeply tiered, giving every pitch a grandstand outlook across the outer Moray Firth. On a clear day, the view takes in the coasts of Caithness and Sutherland. At night, many lights can be picked out including flares of a gas field. The level touring pitches are set in a line across the hill, some separated by trees. Play equipment covers a wide age range. Near Banff, you can visit Duff House, which commands the lower River Deveron, and enjoy its woodland walks.

| NA 0.5 | NP 8 | 0 AMP | | |
| WC | | | | MG | MB |

Pub, shop and slipway 2 miles. Sandy beach 3 miles.

££££ 🐕 ♂♀ M CL CS ⓘ WiFi

Directions: From Macduff, take A98 towards Fraserburgh for 1 mile. Turn left onto the Coastal Trail B9031 for 1.25 miles to the clearly sp site.

GPS: N57°39.710' W002°26.212'
OS grid: 29 NJ 740 636

April - October

Blackpott Cottages CS 〔18〕

Whitehills, Banff, AB45 2JN
Tel: 01261 861396

This small, level, lawned paddock provides splendid sea views. The site is surrounded by a low stone wall which obscures the adjacent road from view when looking out across the narrow rocky beach to the sea. Campers require their own sanitation. There is a fishmonger and a fish and chip shop in the village.

| NA 0.75 | NP 5 | 0 AMP | | |
| WC | | | | MG | MB |

Beach adjacent. Slipway in village.

££££ 🐕 ♂♀ M CL CS ⓘ WiFi

Directions: Travel 1 mile west from Banff on A98, then turn right onto B9038 to Whitehills village centre. At the crossroads turn right sp 'P Harbour Play Park'. Follow the road for 0.5 miles to the end of the small peninsula. The CS is on the right past a static caravan park.

GPS: N57°40.817' W002°34.233'
OS grid: 29 NJ 659 657

April - October

Banff Links Caravan Park

Banff, Aberdeenshire, Grampian, AB45 2JJ
Tel: 01261 812228
www.aberdeenshire.gov.uk/caravanparks/locations/banff.asp

Perfectly located, this level site is right next to Banff village with all its amenities. Some static and 28 touring pitches are right on the waterfront on the top of the pebble bank. Front row tourers have a great view in one area. In another terraced area, the vista is good, too. When the tide is out, a large sandy beach is exposed that is great for children, and Boyndie Bay is also a popular surfing spot. All pitches have electricity.

| NA 3.5 | NP 62 | 10 AMP | | |

| WC | | | | | | MG | MB |

Slipway at Banff.

£££ 🐕 👫 M CL CS (i) WiFi

Directions: From Banff, travel west on A98 for 0.5 miles. Turn right towards the sea sp 'Banff Links' with the campsite symbol. Drive straight for 500m to the sea. The campsite is clearly sp.

GPS: N57°40.152' W002°33.210'
OS grid: 29 NJ 670 646

April - October

Sandend Caravan Park

Sandend, Portsoy, Aberdeenshire,
AB45 2UA Tel: 01261 842660
www.sandendcaravanpark.co.uk

This site is set in a conservation village and overlooks the gorgeous, flat, golden, sandy beach of Sandend Bay. The site is level throughout but many of the pitches have wonderful sea views and everything is neat and tidy. 20 pitches have electricity and 5 are hard. There is direct access to the beach from the site and body boarding will amuse children for hours. A footpath goes each way along the coast, and Findlater Castle is a short walk away. For the safety of children, dogs are admitted at the management's discretion.

| NA 4.5 | NP 48 | 10 AMP | | |

| WC | | | | | | MG | MB |

Pub 1 mile. Slipway 1.5 miles in Portsoy.

£££ 🐕 👫 M CL CS (i) WiFi

Directions: 2.5 miles west of Portsoy, turn north off A98 onto a 30mph road to Sandend. The site is on the right in 0.5 miles, adjacent to an old school and a sandy beach.

GPS: N57°40.923' W002°44.923'
OS grid: 29 NJ 555 661

April - October

Portsoy Caravan Park

The Links, Portsoy, Aberdeenshire,
AB45 2RQ Tel: 01261 842695
www.aberdeenshire.gov.uk/caravanparks

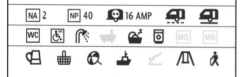

In a sheltered, grassy amphitheatre at the head of Links Bay, the tourers and statics are set in semicircles on the rising ground giving all a fine outlook over the bay framed by rocky headlands. The only 2, adjacent hard pitches are reserved for motorhomes but the ground elsewhere is firm. An hour or two could be spent wandering the streets of attractive, well-kept traditional houses and cottages among which are shops, cafés, an impressive emporium, a community 'thrift' shop and a museum.

NA	2	NP	40	16 AMP		
WC					MG	MB

££££ 🐕 †† Ⓜ CL CS ⓘ WiFi

Directions: In Portsoy turn north off A98 into Church Street sp with the campsite symbol. In 100m turn right into Institute Street. At the T-junction, turn right and immediately fork left into St Comb's Road to the site. The turns are well sp.

GPS: N57°40.967' W002°41.100'
OS grid: 29 NJ 591 660

April - October

Findochty Caravan Park

Jubilee Terrace, Findochty, Buckie, AB56 4QA
Tel: 01542 835303
www.findochtycaravanpark.co.uk

Sheltered from the south, the site is at the head of its own tiny, rock-framed cove. Front row pitches are just above the pebble beach with free space allowing the second and slightly higher third row to see to the distant North Sea horizon. Eider ducks and oyster catchers nest on the nearby rock stack. The swell breaks on outlying rocks in snow white clouds of foam. Of the mostly level pitches, 24 are on hardstanding and 26 have electricity. Motorhomes need a short hose to drain wastewater, and booking should be made for those over 7.5m in length. The coast path runs each way from the site. Yachts and inshore fishing boats crowd the adjacent harbour, with a restaurant just around the corner from the site.

NA	3	NP	30	16 AMP		
WC					MG	MB

££££ 🐕 †† Ⓜ CL CS ⓘ WiFi

Directions: To avoid a steep, twisting, narrow descent into Findochty when coming from the east, approach from Buckie. On A98 from Fochabers, turn left onto A942 into Buckie. Turn right and continue along the coast road. On entering Findochty, take the fine left fork down School Hill. Turn 1st left into Jubilee Terrace, passing the harbour to the site. Signing is good. Reception is outside the entrance.

GPS: N57°41.882' W002°54.487'
OS grid: 28 NJ 459 679

March - October

Strathlene Caravan Site

Great Eastern Road, Strathlene, Portessie,
Buckie, Moray, AB56 1SR
Tel: 01542 834851

Many of the pitches, which are mostly hard, offer views across the coast road and beach to the sea and the Sutherland coast. The touring pitches, all of which have electricity, are situated centrally with statics on three sides. The sandy beach with rock patches is backed by pebbles. A café is situated directly across the road from the site, and plenty of shops and restaurants can be found in nearby Buckie, which is a major fishing port. Seafood shops and restaurants are therefore numerous.

| NA 3 | NP 27 | 16 AMP | | |

| WC | | | | | | MG | MB |

Pub and shops 1.5 miles.

£££ £

Directions: The site is beside the Moray Coast Trail A942, 1 mile west of Findochty and just east of the Buckie-Gordonsburg-Portessie conurbation. It is well sp.

GPS: N57°41.279' W002°55.730'
OS grid: 28 NJ 448 669

April - October

Spey Bay Golf

Spey Bay, Nr Fochabers, Moray, IV32 7PJ
Tel: 01343 820424
www.speybay.co

Despite having no electricity, lawned pitches close behind the shingle bank at the top of the beach are popular for the sea view northwards. Other pitches all have electricity. The campsite and the golf facilities are run jointly. The site was effectively new in 2012, sharing new washroom facilities to high modern standards with the golf club. The bar and lounge are open to campers, who receive advantageous rates on the golf course. The Speyside Way passes the site and the Scottish Dolphin Centre is nearby.

| NA 2.5 | NP 30 | 16 AMP | | |

| WC | | | | | | MG | MB |

£££ £

Directions: From Fochabers, take B9104 to Spey Bay. The site is on the right as you reach the sea at a left bend in the road.

GPS: N57°40.300' W003°05.060'
OS grid: 28 NJ 354 651

April - October

Burghead Beach Caravan Park

25

Burghead, Elgin, Morayshire, IV30 5RP
Tel: 01343 830084
www.lossiemouthcaravans.co.uk/burghead.asp

This site, mainly for statics, has just 1 pitch with an outstanding view along the bay to Burghead Harbour. Laid out in front of you across the Moray Firth is the Sutherland coast with the Sutors of Cromarty directly opposite. 3 or 4 pitches in a central group of 10 allow a sea view between statics. 5 more pitches are sheltered at the forest edge. All are on level, hard grass and have electricity. The beach is sandy, and the adjacent Roseisle Forest has a path to Findhorn.

NA 1.5 NP 16 16 AMP

WC MG MB

££££ M CL CS WiFi

Directions: From Elgin, take B9013 to Burghead. Just into the town, look out for a football field on the left. Beyond it, turn left into Bridge Street sp 'Caravan Park'. Follow this to the site.

GPS: N57°41.928' W003°29.297'
OS grid: 28 NJ 114 686

mid February - mid January

Station Caravan Park

26

West Beach, Hopeman, Moray, IV30 5RU
Tel: 01343 830880
www.stationcaravanpark.co.uk

The site's touring pitches are in three distinct areas. From several pitches on a grassed mound on the old platform, you can see between well-spaced statics to the Moray Firth. From a higher paddock at the far end of the site, some pitches gain limited views to the sea. The third, sunken, walled area is a quiet, sheltered sun trap. Most pitches have electricity. Users of very large units should book in advance. The sandy beach, harbour, shops and services are close by in the village and the Coastal Path passes by.

NA 13 NP 45 16 AMP

WC MG MB

££££ M CL CS WiFi

Directions: Between Burghead and Lossiemouth, at Hopeman on B9012, turn north on Harbour Road. The site is at the end on the left near the harbour.

Scottish Tourist Board ★★★★ Holiday Park

GPS: N57°42.537' W003°26.268'
OS grid: 28 NJ 143 696

April - October

Fortrose Caravan Park

Wester Greengates, Fortrose,
Ross-shire, IV10 8RX
Tel: 01381 621927

The site's location on the shoreline provides interesting, panoramic views across the Moray Firth, including moored sailing craft, the distant hills and a suspension road bridge. This is a beautiful site that is mostly level and has a quiet road running through it. Footpaths provide for interesting walking to Chanonry Point where dolphins may be seen, and along by the shore to Rosemarkie. Even when an easterly wind drives noisy surf onto Rosemarkie beach, you can find shelter and a smoother sea here.

NA	3	NP	50	16 AMP		

Shop 10 mins walk. Slipway in harbour.

£££

Directions: From A832 in Fortrose, turn opposite the Bank of Scotland into Academy Street. The site is on the right in 0.5 miles.

GPS: N57°34.717' W004°07.107'
OS grid: 27 NH 734 562

Easter - October

Rosemarkie Camping and Caravanning Club Site

Ness Road East, Rosemarkie, Fortrose,
Highlands, IV10 8SE Tel: 01381 621117
www.campingandcaravanningclub.co.uk

This is a very attractive level site on the shore of a half-moon bay with beautiful views out into the Moray Firth and across to Fort George. Pitches in the front row beside the mostly pebble beach have magnificent, unobstructed views, but have no electricity and the surf can be noisy. Bottlenose dolphins are seen on most days from Chanonry Point and sometimes even from the site. The Fortrose and Rosemarkie Golf Course is next door. Walk 0.5 miles to Rosemarkie and, from the play area and café at the far end of the village, try the wooded burnside walk, strolling back through the interesting village, where there is a regular bus service to Inverness.

NA	6	NP	60	16 AMP		

Pub and shop 10 mins walk.

£££

Directions: From A832 in Fortrose, turn southeast by the Police Station down Ness Road. After 0.5 miles, at the caravan sign, turn left along Ness Road East to the site.

GPS: N57°34.997' W004°06.555'
OS grid: 27 NH 739 568

April - October

Seaview Farm Caravan Park

Hilton, Dornoch, Sutherland, IV25 3PW
Tel: 01862 810294

This is an ideal, quiet little site similar to CLs and CSs. Sheltering trees still allow some pitches a view across the Dornoch Firth to Tain. The tiny amenity block has 3 toilets with washbasins and a sink for washing dishes and clothes by hand. A short walk leads to a sandy beach and the coast path to Dornoch, which has shops and other services. Excellent panels in the streets illustrate the town's history.

| NA 2.5 | NP 15 | 💀 16 AMP | | |

Pub and shop 1.25 miles. Slipway and pool 1.5 miles.

££££ 🐕 ♟ M CL CS ⓘ WiFi

Directions: From A9, take A949 to Dornoch, then an unclassified road north towards Embo. After 1.5 miles, turn right sp 'High Croft B&B' for 200m to the site entrance. Call at the house named 'Seaview' 200m further on.

GPS: N57°53.845' W004°00.896'
OS grid: 21 NH 807 915

June - September

Dornoch Caravan and Camping Park

The Links, Dornoch, Sutherland, IV25 3LX
Tel: 01862 810423
www.dornochcaravans.co.uk

This is a large dunes site, but many pitches have space to themselves in individual mown lawns or in small groups surrounded by natural dune grassland. Only a few tent pitches offer direct sea views, but the popular sandy beach is just a few metres away. Most pitches are level and have electricity. One of several, the main facilities building is immaculately fitted out. A few mins walk is the centre of the Royal Burgh of Dornoch surrounded by historic buildings including the cathedral. The Royal Dornoch championship golf course adjoins the site, and nearby Dunrobin Castle deserves a day's visit.

| NA 25 | NP 120 | 💀 10/16 AMP | | |

Slipway 3.5 miles.

£££ 🐕 ♟ M CL CS ⓘ WiFi

Directions: Enter Dornoch on A949 and continue along the main road. Turn right at the sharp left-hand bend in the town centre. Follow winding Church Street for 0.5 miles to the site.

GPS: N57°52.595' W004°01.322'
OS grid: 21 NH 803 892

April - October

Grannie's Helian Hame

Embo, Dornoch, Sutherland,
Highlands, IV25 3QD   Tel: 01862 810383
www.parkdeanholidays.co.uk

In this large Parkdean Holidays site, tourers occupy a peninsula near the extensive sandy beach with some rock. Many pitches here have some view of the Dornoch Firth. Tents pitch by the shore or among the dunes. All pitches are level and on grass except for 8 that are hard and fully serviced. A further 84 have electricity. This family site has an abundance of facilities and entertainment, including a large play area, adventure playground, indoor heated pool, restaurant, takeaway, bar, entertainment, sauna, tennis, and crazy golf. Nearby are the Royal Dornoch Golf Club and several distilleries that welcome visitors.

NA	5	NP	185	☠	13 AMP		
WC	♿	🚿	🛁	🚰	⚫	MG	MB

Slipway on site.

£££ £   🐕 ††   M   CL   CS   ⓘ   WiFi

Directions: 3 miles north of Dornoch Firth Bridge, turn right off A9 onto A949 to Dornoch. In the town centre, follow the main road as it bends left, sp for the site. After 2.25 miles, turn right to Embo following the main route and sp 'Embo Pier' into the site.

Scottish TOURIST BOARD ★★★★ HOLIDAY PARK

GPS: N57°54.463' W003°59.825'
OS grid: 21 NH 818 926

March - October

Crakaig Seaside Caravan Park

Loth, Helmsdale, Sutherland, KW8 6HP
Tel: 01408 621260

The extensive site is spread across the grassy coastal slope above a beach of sand and rock, so all pitches have a clear view out over the North Sea. The many seasonal caravans are not simultaneously occupied and the atmosphere is peaceful. Camp fires are allowed and sheep may be on the land. Water is available but no electricity. The small facility block provides toilets, showers and dishwashing. A small area at one extreme end of the beach is available to naturists.

NA	40	NP	25	☠	0 AMP		
WC	♿	🚿	🛁	🚰	⚫	MG	MB

Pub, shop and slipway 6 miles.

££ ££   🐕 ††   M   CL   CS   ⓘ   WiFi

Directions: From Brora, take A9 for 5.5 miles. 0.75 miles beyond the Loth River bridge, turn right down a minor road and call at the 1st house on the left. Continue down the same narrow road, past a downhill hairpin bend, to an arched railway bridge (max height 3.2m/10ft 6in, width 2.82m/9ft 3in). The site is beyond. Users of large units can use hardstanding before the bridge.

GPS: N58°04.427' W003°46.200'
OS grid: 17 NC 957 106

April - October

Inver Caravan Park

Houstry Road, Dunbeath, Caithness,
KW6 6EH Tel: 01593 731441
www.inver-caravan-park.co.uk

Several pitches give a splendid view along the steep coast to Dunbeath Castle and out across the North Sea to wind turbines and the flares of gas platforms. This small, well-kept site has magnificent facilities that include a drying room and a large shower room for families and the disabled. The site is situated high above the sea. A 5 to 10 mins walk down a rather steep path leads to the beach. A longer walk of about 0.25 miles gives an easier descent. A circular walk from the site takes in pretty Dunbeath Strath.

NA	1	NP	15	☠ 16 AMP	🔌	🔌
WC	♿	🚿	🛁	🍼	⊙	MG	MB

Pub 350m. Shop 0.5 miles. Slipway in village.

£££ 🐕 ♟ M CL CS ⓘ WiFi

Directions: The site is situated near A9 on the northern outskirts of Dunbeath. Turn northwest sp 'Houstry' and 'Inver Caravan Park'. The site is on the left in 50m.

GPS: N58°15.025' W003°25.267'
OS grid: 11 ND 166 299

All Year

John O'Groats Camping and Caravan Site

John O'Groats, Caithness, Highlands,
KW1 4YR Tel: 01955 611329
www.johnogroatscampsite.co.uk

On a low cliff above the rocky shore, all pitches in the front row have a fine panorama of the notorious Pentland Firth, one of the most dangerous shipping channels in the world. The view takes in Stroma to the west and from Scapa Flow to the Pentland Skerries and Duncansby Head Lighthouse in the east. Many species of seabird fly past, and grey seals are often seen close to the beach. All the hardstanding pitches are in the front field which is separated by a high bank from a second of similar size. Wildlife cruises depart from John O'Groats' tiny harbour adjacent to the site.

NA	4	NP	90	☠ 16 AMP	🔌	🔌
WC	♿	🚿	🛁	🍼	⊙	MG	MB

Pub and shop 0.5 miles. Slipway adjacent.

£££ 🐕 ♟ M CL CS ⓘ WiFi

Directions: The site is situated at the end of the A99 on the right.

GPS: N58°38.613' W003°04.098'
OS grid: 12 ND 382 733

April - September

Kittiwake Cottage *CL*

Scarfskerry, Thurso, Caithness,
KW14 8XN
Tel: 01847 851718

Distant views of Dunnet Head to the west, Orkney to the north, and Stroma to the east are seen across fields from this quiet *CL* in a scattered community typical of crofting landscapes. Two level lawns provide 5 pitches, but 2 or 3 motorhomes can stand on driveways as necessary. Ducks and hens give a greeting. The shore in this area is rocky, with a small harbour at Harrow. Nearby Castle of Mey, home of the late Queen Mother, can be seen from the site. It provides an excellent guided tour, gardens and a café.

| NA 0.5 | NP 5 | 0 AMP | | |

| WC | | | | | | MG | MB |

Pub, beach and slipway 1 mile. Shop 9 miles at Castletown.

£££ M *CL* CS (i) WiFi

Directions: From Thurso, take A836 eastwards for 7 miles beyond Castletown. Turn left sp 'Scarfskerry', then right at a T-junction. After 1 mile, the *CL* is well sp on the left.

GPS: N58°39.118' W003°14.910'
OS grid: 12 ND 276 745

All year

Wheems Bothies and Campsite

Eastside, South Ronaldsay, Orkney,
KW17 2TJ Tel: 01856 831556
www.wheemsorganic.co.uk

From its hillside vantage point, this informal site's view is of Orkney's typically impressive cliffs and the open North Sea towards Norway. Pitching areas are mown amid longer grass on a gentle slope. Electricity is supplied to 3 pitches. In addition to there being camping pods, a yurt serves as recreation space or emergency accommodation for campers. Caravans and motorhomes not longer than 6m are accepted if ground conditions permit: phone in advance to check. Permanent buildings include a semi-enclosed kitchen and dishwashing area, a small block with toilets, and simple showers. A small craft gallery is part of the establishment.

| NA 1.5 | NP 20 | 5 AMP | | |

| WC | | | | | | MG | MB |

Pub, shop and slipway 2 miles. Beach 0.75 miles.

££££ M *CL* CS (i) WiFi

Directions: From A961 close to St Margaret's Hope, 100m southwest of the junction with Church Street, take the minor road southeast for 1.25 miles to a minor crossroads. Continue ahead for 300m, then turn left sp 'Camping Wheems' up a narrow lane to the site.

GPS: N58°48.471' W002°55.613'
OS grid: 7 ND 466 916

April - October

Deerness Community Centre Caravan and Campsite

37

Deerness, Orkney, KW17 2QH
Tel: 01856 741317

The sea is only distantly seen, but this gem of a site is provided by a hospitable community. It has 10 tent pitches on grass and 10 level pitches for caravans and motorhomes on asphalt, 4 with electricity. Tenters are given access to the immaculately kept toilets and a kitchen, whereas caravanners and motorhomers need to make individual arrangements. Note that the nearest toilet emptying point is at the campsite in Kirkwall. Walks can be taken on a nature reserve 3 miles away.

NA	1	NP	20			

No toilet emptying point on site. Pub 4 miles. Shop 0.5 miles. Beach 1.25 miles. Slipway 1 mile.

££££ 🐕 †† M CL CS (i) WiFi

Directions: From Kirkwall, take A960 to its end, then B9050 for 1 mile to the community centre on the left.

GPS: N58°56.195' W002°44.826'
OS grid: 6 HY 571 057

All year

Sumburgh Hotel

38

Sumburgh, Shetland, ZE3 9JN
Tel: 01950 460201
www.sumburghhotel.com

A fine sea view over the West Voe of Sumburgh to craggy cliffs is the the reward for staying at the extreme southern tip of Shetland where sea birds nest in huge numbers. Beside the imposing hotel is an asphalt area with hook-ups and water taps. The hotel's toilets are available by day, but chemical emptying is not provided for. The hotel offers service washes. Close by are a wide sandy beach and the Jarlshof archaeological site. Up near the lighthouse is an observation point for watching those cliff-nesting birds.

NA	0.25	NP	5			

Shop 1.5 miles.

££££ 🐕 †† M CL CS (i) WiFi

Directions: From Lerwick, take A970 to its end beyond Sumburgh Airport. The gateway to the hotel is just ahead on the right.

GPS: N59°52.295' W001°17.257'
OS grid: 4 HU 399 096

All year

Ness Boating Club

Eastshore, Virkie, Shetland, ZE3 9JS
Tel: 01950 460712
www.nessbc.shetland.co.uk

The hospitable club welcomes caravans and motorhomes to park near its marina in the Pool of Virkie and look out over the open sea. Close at hand, the harbour dries out to leave mudflats that are visited by many bird species. Busy Sumburgh Airport directly across the Pool provides further interest. Pitches are level and hard, with 4 hook-ups. Basic CL-type services are available. The club plans to provide further facilities.

| NA | 0.25 | NP | 10 | | 16 AMP | | |

Shop 0.75 miles. Sandy beach 1.5 miles.

££££ 🐕 ♟ M CL CS ⓘ WiFi

Directions: From Lerwick, take A970 until Sumburgh Airport is in sight. Turn left to the site on the right, sp 'Eastshore', and follow road for 0.75 miles.

GPS: N59°53.120' W001°17.107'
OS grid: 4 HU 402 113

All year

Levenwick Campsite

Taingview, Levenwick, Shetland, ZE2 9HX
Tel: 01950 422320
www.levenwick.weebly.com

This must be one of the best campsites in the Northern Isles for an impressive sea view. From a high vantage point you can look over Levenwick village and across to Crumlewick Ness, No Ness, and out to sea. Facilities are provided at the adjacent community hall. 12 level pitches for tents have a little shelter. The 5 asphalt touring pitches are almost level. 9 hook-ups are provided. Extra facilities include a little dining room with a microwave oven for tenters. Buses pass the site. A sandy bay is a modest walk away. Boat trips run to the Island of Mousa to see its substantial broch and the storm petrels that nest there.

| NA | 0.5 | NP | 17 | | 16 AMP | | |

Shop 0.5 miles. Beach 1 mile. Pub and slipway 5 miles.

££££ 🐕 ♟ M CL CS ⓘ WiFi

Directions: From Lerwick, take A970 for 16 miles. The hall and site are clearly sp on the left beside the road.

GPS: N59°58.370' W001°16.595'
OS grid: 4 HU 405 211

May - September

Bridge End Outdoor Centre

Bridge End, Burra, Shetland, ZE2 9LD
Tel: 01595 745301
http://bridgeendoutdoor.com

Photo courtesy of Finlay MacBeath

Among a complex of long peninsulas that form part of the western mainland lies the sea loch of South Voe. At its head is an isthmus on which stands a community-run outdoor centre, from which there is a long, sea-level view. It is a delightful, sheltered spot with boating facilities amid a scattering of croft houses. Camping is free, but £5 is charged if you wish to use the facilities.

| NA | 0.25 | NP | 32 | | 16 AMP | | |

Beach 1.5 miles. Pub and shop 2 miles. Slipway on site.

££££ 🐕 †† M CL CS ⓘ WiFi

Directions: From Scalloway, take B9074 almost to Hamnavoe, then turn left onto the minor road southwards for 1.75 miles sp 'Bridge End'. Fork left downhill to the conspicuous centre.

GPS: N60°04.903' W001°19.855'
OS grid: 4 HU 373 331

All year

Oot Ower Lounge

Livister, Whalsay, Shetland, ZE2 9AQ
Tel: 01806 566575

From this high location, views extend over most of Whalsay, including the distant sea, and the trout-stocked loch close by. A tapestry of wild flowers lines the roads, and other fishing lochs abound. Its central position makes the family-run lounge and its bar a hub for the area. A fine leisure centre is just 0.5 miles away and Symbister has a well stocked shop. The site has plenty of space for tents and a clean, level asphalt surface for caravans and motorhomes.

| NA | 0.5 | NP | 4 | | 13 AMP | | |

Shop 0.5 miles. Slipway 1.5 miles. Shingle beach 2 miles.

£££ 🐕 †† M CL CS ⓘ WiFi

Directions: From the ferry terminal at Symbister, follow road around harbour and turn east sp 'Isbister'. Continue east for 1 mile and Oot Ower is above the road on the left, opposite Huxter Loch.

GPS: N60°20.616' W000°59.563'
OS grid: 2 HU 557 626

All year

Whalsay Golf Club

Skaw, Brough, Whalsay, Shetland, ZE2 9AW
Tel: 01806 566705
www.whalsaygolfclub.co.uk

High up at Skaw on the northeastern extremity of Whalsay is the northernmost golf course in Britain. Parking or camping around the clubhouse gives a wide view out over the North Sea, including the island of Fetlar if visibility allows. Along with the sheep, any number of tents can be accommodated providing that they are not actually on the course! A dozen motorhomes or caravans could be distributed on 7 level asphalt spaces and an additional grassy area. Electricity is supplied for 2, and the excellent facilities of the clubhouse are available. The loch beside the club and others elsewhere offer trout fishing.

NA	0.5	NP	12				
WC						MG	MB

Pebble beach 0.5 miles. Shop and slipway 6 miles.

££££ 🐕 ♀♂ M CL CS ⓘ WiFi

Directions: From Symbister ferry terminal, drive northeast along the west coast of Whalsay for 5 miles. The golf club is at the road end.

GPS: N60°22.793' W000°55.470'
OS grid: 2 HU 594 667

All year

Burravoe Caravan Site

Burravoe Marina, Neepaback, Burravoe,
Yell, Shetland, ZE2 9AY
Tel: 01957 722315

Directly behind and above the marina, all the terraced, hard pitches have a 180° view across the sheltered upper reach of Burra Voe to the peninsula of Heoga Ness. Walk around the Voe or northeast to the nearby rocky shore and cliffs to watch gannets and terns diving and puffins, black guillemots and others fishing from the surface. In the village, visit the Old Haa exhibition. A discarded 36ft lifeboat from SS Canberra, a gift to the Pier Trust, made a perfect roof for a fine modern toilet block: it must be one of the most smartly appointed in Shetland.

NA	0.5	NP	10		16 AMP		
WC						MG	MB

Shop 0.5 miles. Beach 2 miles. Pub 7 miles.

££££ 🐕 ♀♂ M CL CS ⓘ WiFi

Directions: From the Ulsta ferry terminal on Yell, take B9081 for 4.5 miles to Burravoe. From the hairpin bend in the village turn southeast sp 'Burravoe', then 'Brunthill', 'Burravoe Pier' and 'Neepabank'. Pass to the left of a church, then turn 1st left sp 'Neepabank' and 'Burravoe Pier' to the site.

GPS: N60°29.850' W001°02.667'
OS grid: 2 HU 526 797

All year

Gardiesfauld Youth Hostel

Uyeasound, Unst, Shetland, ZE2 9DW
Tel: 01957 755279
www.gardiesfauld.shetland.co.uk

All 5 of the level, hard pitches have a sea-level view along Uyea Sound to the right and Skuda Sound to the left. Salmon cages, ubiquitous hereabouts, are in each sound, and attendant boats are frequently on the move. A small-boat harbour adjoins the beach of sand and stones in front of the site. Otters are frequently seen and seabirds abound. Nearby Baltasound is said to have been the biggest herring processing station in Europe. Unst Boat Haven and Unst Heritage Centre have absorbing displays. The site has no chemical disposal point. Sheltered tent spaces are beside the hostel. Facilities are in the hostel, but a small, clean public toilet is beside the pitches.

| NA 0.25 | NP 5 | | | |

Slipway 0.5 miles. Pub and shop 8 miles.

££££ 🐕 ♦♦ M CL CS ⓘ WiFi

Directions: From Belmont ferry terminal on Unst, take A968 for 2 miles. Turn right onto B9084 sp 'Uyeasound'. The hostel is on the right in 0.5 miles.

GPS: N60°41.302' W000°55.130'
OS grid: 1 HP 591 010

April - October

Cullivoe Hall

Cullivoe, Yell, Shetland, ZE2 9DD
Tel: 01957 744380

The parking area offers a distant but spectacular view across the entrance to Bluemull Sound to islets and cliffs on which the swell breaks. Essential services are all provided beside the pitches. A short distance away is a fine beach and more impressive cliffs, also the memorial recording a 19th century fishing tragedy. Cullivoe Hall is also a hostel with full facilities that are available to visitors when there is spare capacity.

| NA 0.75 | NP 15 | 16 AMP | | |

Slipway 1 mile. Beach 1.5 miles.

££££ 🐕 ♦♦ M CL CS ⓘ WiFi

Directions: From the ferry terminal at Ulsta on Yell, take A968 for about 17 miles to a crossroads at Gutcher, then B9082 to Cullivoe. The hall is beside this road in the village.

GPS: N60°42.403' W001°00.733'
OS grid: 1 HP 540 030

All year

North Roe and Lochend Hall

Skoe Knowe, North Roe, Shetland,
ZE2 9RY
Tel: 01806 533276

Photo courtesy of Finlay MacBeath

In front of the hall are 12 spacious asphalt pitches with electricity, all enjoying the distant view across the enclosed bay of Burra Voe, which faces out onto the sound of Yell. Many more units can be accommodated either at the hall or across the road when rallies or festivals are taking place. The hall's modern facilities are available to visitors by arrangement with the hall representative who calls to see visitors. Short walks reveal the spectacular coastal scenery that surrounds the only campsite on this remote peninsula.

NA	1	NP	15	16 AMP

WC · 16 AMP · MG · MB

Slipway 1.5 miles. Sandy beach 2 miles. Shop 5 miles. Pub 8 miles.

£££ · M · CL · CS · i · WiFi

Directions: From Tingwall, take A970 north approximately 17 miles to Brae. After a further 7 miles, fork right to North Roe. After another 8 miles the hall will be on the right beside the road.

GPS: N60°34.345' W001°19.968'
OS grid: 1 HU 367 878

All year

Braewick Café and Caravan Park

Braewick, Eshaness, Shetland, ZE2 9RS
Tel: 01806 503345
www.eshaness.shetland.co.uk

Photo courtesy of Mark Hughes

From the elevated site at Eshaness on the western tip of the 'mainland', the view extends across Braewick along the fragmented cliffs and sea stacks with the vicious-looking, teeth-like stacks of the Drongs out at sea. The wide asphalt pitches are equipped with a mains outlet, light, tap, and drain. 4 also have a motorhome waste drain set in the pitch surface. Space for many tents is supplemented by 4 camping pods. Immaculate public toilets, accessible directly from the pitches day and night, are part of the adjacent café and licensed restaurant, where crafts and artwork are on sale. Displays explain the distinctive geology of the region.

NA	1	NP	10	16 AMP

WC · 16 AMP · MG · MB

Shop 3 miles.

£££ · M · CL · CS · i · WiFi

Directions: From Tingwall, take A970 north approximately 17 miles to Brae. After a further 7 miles, fork left to the west. Follow the road for 3.25 miles, then turn right onto B9078. The café and campsite will be on the left in 3 miles.

Scottish TOURIST BOARD ★★★★ TOURING PARK

GPS: N60°29.642' W001°33.442'
OS grid: 3 HU 244 790

March - September

Delting Boating Club

Hillswick Road, Brae, Shetland, ZE2 9QG
Tel: 01806 522524
www.deltingboatingclub.co.uk

From level pitches, all with electricity, distributed along the waterfront, the view takes in the village of Brae set around the head of Busta Voe and extends seaward past Hevden Ness to the islands of Linga and Papa Little. As temporary members of the club, visiting caravanners and motorhomers have the use of the facilities and bar. The club is a hive of activity with windsurfing and sailing courses and sub-aqua activities. A magnificent leisure centre with a swimming pool is only 0.5 miles away. At Muckle Roe, one can walk or take a boat trip to admire the dramatic cliff scenery or see the First World War defences.

| NA | 1 | NP | 13 | 16 AMP | | |

| WC | | | | | | MG | MB |

Shop and sandy beach 0.5 miles.

££££ 🐕 †† M CL CS ⓘ WiFi

Directions: From the pronounced bend of A970 in the centre of Brae village, take A970 westwards for 0.5 miles to the site on the left.

GPS: N60°23.600' W001°21.857'
OS grid: 3 HU 353 679

All year

Skeld Caravan Park and Campsite

Harbour View, Wester Skeld, Skeld, Shetland, ZE2 9NL Tel: 01595 860287
www.skeldcaravanpark.co.uk

In the Skeld district of the western 'mainland', this community-run marina and campsite is situated at the head of Skelda Voe. 2 pitches have a wonderful view right down the voe, with a beach immediately below where otters are frequently seen. Other pitches look over the marina and across the voe to the hills beyond. The tent field adjoins the smart facilities building that includes a full kitchen and a dining and dishwashing room primarily for tenters.

| NA | 3.5 | NP | 34 | 16 AMP | | |

| WC | | | | | | MG | MB |

Sandy beach 0.25 miles.

££££ 🐕 †† M CL CS ⓘ WiFi

Directions: From Tingwall, take A971 for 11.5 miles to Bixter. After another 1.4 miles, turn left onto B9071 for 7 miles to Wester Skeld, where the marina is clearly visible.

GPS: N60°11.175' W001°26.383'
OS grid: 4 HU 312 447

All year

Ayre's Rock Campsite

Ayre's Rock, Sanday, Orkney, KW17 2AY
Tel: 01857 600410
www.ayres-rock-sanday-orkney.co.uk

On the northwest coast of the island of Sanday, this small, very slightly sloping grass site has a sea view northwards past other bays, headlands, and islets. The first bay has a sandy beach a few mins walk away. The site also has camping pods and a hostel with 8 beds. The island offers visitors excellent birdwatching, fishing, archaeology and Second World War military installations. Various festivals take place throughout the year. An enthralling introductory tour of the island, conducted by resident experts, takes place each Wednesday throughout the summer.

| NA 0.5 | NP 9 | 10 AMP | | |
| WC | | | | |

Shop 0.5 miles. Pub 2.5 miles.

££££ 🐕 ✝✝ M CL CS ⓘ WiFi

Directions: From the Sanday ferry terminal, take B9070 for 5.75 miles to a right-angle bend in the road sp to the hostel. Here, fork left for 0.5 miles to the site. A bus service for foot passengers meets each ferry.

GPS: N59°15.344' W002°36.688'
OS grid: 5 HY 652 412

All year

Sand O' Gill

Pierowall, Isle of Westray, Orkney, KW17 2DN
Tel: 01857 677374

The site is situated at the head of a wide, sweeping bay behind a long arc of the sandy beach. This quiet site is L-shaped and undulating but generally level, with well-drained grass and 4 hook-ups. The view takes in the scene above. In 2012 the site gained a new, small, well-equipped toilet block that includes a laundry room. The owners of the associated B&B are hospitable and obliging. Owners of long motorhomes or very long caravans should note the tight turn at the entrance. In one direction along the bay is the terminal for the passenger ferry to Papa Westray. In the other direction are shops, a heritage centre, and a swimming pool.

| NA 0.75 | NP 10 | 13 AMP | | |
| WC | | | | MG | MB |

Slipway 0.25 miles. Pub and shop 0.5 miles.

££££ 🐕 ✝✝ M CL CS ⓘ WiFi

Directions: From the Rapness ferry terminal at the south of Westray, take B9066 for 7.5 miles to Pierowall. The well sp entrance lane to the site is on the left, beyond the B&B house.

GPS: N59°19.636' W002°58.938'
OS grid: 5 HY 442 494

April - September

The Barn Hostel and Campsite

Chalmersquoy, Westray, Orkney, KW17 2BZ
Tel: 01857 677214
www.thebarnwestray.com

Most pitches offer a sea view northwards across the wide Bay of Pierowall to Gill Pier at the far end of the village. Seals can often be seen on rocks not far away. The grass pitches on both fields all have electricity and are almost level. Heavy motorhomes could park on hard areas nearby if conditions require. Facilities include cookers, microwave oven, dishwashing and a dining room primarily for tenters. A drying room and games room are also provided. Dogs are admitted only by prior arrangement. Beef farming and commercial fishing are much in evidence but Whalsay also has exciting bird and plant populations.

| NA 1 | NP 13 | 16 AMP | | |

| WC | | | | | | MG | MB |

Shop 0.5 miles. Beach 1 mile. Slipway 1.5 miles.

££££ 🐕 †† M CL CS ⓘ WiFi

Directions: From the Rapness ferry terminal at the south of Westray, take B9066 for 6.75 miles to Pierowall. The site is on the left at a left-hand bend upon reaching the seafront.

GPS: N59°18.881' W002°59.022'
OS grid: 5 HY 441 480

All year

Rousay Hostel and Campsite

Trumland Farm, Rousay, Orkney, KW17 2PU
Tel: 01856 821252

Photo courtesy of Carol Ray

The hostel and campsite are on rising ground 0.25 miles from the shore and overlook Wyre Sound with views to Orkney mainland and the islands of Egilsay and Wyre and more distant islands. 1 or 2 motorhomes or a caravan are sometimes accommodated on hard ground, though not necessarily with a direct sea view: enquire before travelling. Dogs by arrangement only. Cycles can be hired to ride the 15 mile circuit of the island. Archaeological features abound on the island, with a continuing excavation in progress. An information-packed visitor centre is located near the ferry pier.

| NA 0.25 | NP 5 | 0 AMP | | |

| WC | | | | | | MG | MB |

Pub and slipway 0.5 miles. Shop 3 miles.

££££ 🐕 †† M CL CS ⓘ WiFi

Directions: From the Rousay ferry terminal, follow the main road uphill. Turn left at the war memorial and at a T-junction. The hostel and campsite are on the left after 0.25 miles.

GPS: N59°07.883' W002°59.860'
OS grid: 6 HY 430 276

All year

Birsay
Outdoor Centre and Campsite `55`

Birsay, Orkney, KW17 2LY
Tel: 01856 873535 Ext. 2430
www.orkney.gov.uk

Associated with Birsay Outdoor Centre Hostel and a new leisure centre is this neat campsite with well-kept grass pitches. The immaculate facilities are housed in modern portable buildings. A kitchen and drying room are accessible in the hostel building. Parts of the site have a distant view westwards over the sea. Other parts take in Brough Head and its lighthouse. But these far-off views promise a good outing. A 2-mile drive leads to a car park overlooking the causeway to the island of Brough Head. One can walk up to the lighthouse for a fine sea vista or visit the ancient Pictish and Norse archaeological site.

| NA 3 | NP 20 | 16 AMP | | |

| WC | ♿ | 🚿 | 🛁 | 🚰 | 🔌 | MG | MB |

Bar and shop 1 mile. Slipway 2 miles.

££££ 🐕 †† M CL CS ⓘ WiFi

Directions: From Stromness, take A967 for 12.5 miles to Birsay. Beyond the building sp 'Birsay Outdoor Centre', turn left onto B9056 for 100m to the site.

GPS: N59°07.228' W003°18.407'
OS grid: 6 HY 253 267

April - October

Point of Ness
Caravan and Camping Site `56`

Ness Road, Stromness, Orkney, KW16 1NY
Tel: 01856 850532 Ext. 2430
www.orkney.gov.uk

Surrounded on three sides by the sea, this popular site has a maritime atmosphere. Look one way up Hamnavoe to the busy harbour with the Northlink ferry terminal, fishing boats great and small, and dive boats that take parties to Scapa Flow. Look across to the hilly Stenness area of the 'mainland', or south to the nearby island of Graemsay and beyond to Hoy. On the fourth side is the town's well-used golf course. A walk of 1 mile takes you along the contorted, flagstone-paved main street, with ancient quays and warehouses to one side and steep, narrow closes on the other. Allow half a day when visiting the Stromness Museum.

| NA 2 | NP 35 | 16 AMP | | |

| WC | ♿ | 🚿 | 🛁 | 🚰 | 🔌 | MG | MB |

Pub 0.75 miles. Shop 1 mile.

££££ 🐕 †† M CL CS ⓘ WiFi

Directions: Don't approach through town centre. From north on A965 or A967, at 1st roundabout take 3rd exit onto North End Road. Fork right onto Back Road. At roundabout, take 1st exit. Keep right, then keep left. At seafront turn right and follow sp to site. From ferry, follow Ferry Road north to roundabout. Take 1st exit onto North End Road, then as above.

Scottish
TOURIST BOARD
★★★
TOURING
PARK

GPS: N58°57.163' W003°17.792'
OS grid: 6 HY 255 079

April - September

Dunnet Bay Caravan Club Site [57]

Dunnet, Thurso, Highland, KW14 8XD
Tel: 01847 821319
www.caravanclub.co.uk

Many pitches have glorious views of the sea past sand dunes, and some are right next to the beach. Solitude can be enjoyed here whilst you look out over uninterrupted clean-washed sands to Dunnet Head, the northernmost point of mainland Britain. Climbing Dunnet will reward you with magnificent views over the Pentland Firth to Orkney, Ben Loyal and Ben Hope. Users of units over 8.5m/28ft should contact the site in advance. Seadrift Visitor Centre on the site illustrates local wild life.

| NA 5 | NP 57 | 16 AMP | | |

| WC | | | | | | MG | MB |

Pub 0.5 miles. Shop 2.5 miles. Boats can be launched from the beach.

£££

Directions: Travelling from the east (John O'Groats) on A836, the site is on the right, 0.5 miles past Dunnet village. Travelling from the west (Thurso) on A836, the site is on the left 2.5 miles past Castletown.

GPS: N58°36.943' W003°20.732'
OS grid: 12 ND 219 705

April - October

Thurso Bay Caravan and Camping Park [58]

Smith Terrace, Scrabster Road, Thurso, Caithness, KW14 7JY Tel: 01847 892244
www.thursobaycamping.co.uk

The waterside situation gives all pitches a sweeping, unobstructed view across Thurso Bay and the Pentland Firth to the Orkney island of Hoy. Now in private hands, replacing council management, the predominantly grass site slopes very gradually up from the shore. Users of the hard pitches along one boundary need a long hook-up cable. The café/restaurant at reception is large and comfortable. A supermarket is just across the road and all the town's facilities are a few mins walk away. In the same bay, the harbour at Scrabster has a ferry link with Stromness on the Orkney 'mainland'.

| NA 4.5 | NP 72 | 10 AMP | | |

| WC | | | | | | MG | MB |

Slipway 2 miles.

£££

Directions: From the south on A9 or east on A836, cross the river bridge in Thurso. Turn right, then left on A836 westwards. The site is on the right in 0.5 miles.

GPS: N58°35.873' W003°31.793'
OS grid: 12 ND 111 689

April - September

Halladale Inn Caravan Park

Melvich, Sutherland, KW14 7YJ
Tel: 01641 531282
www.halladaleinn.co.uk

The level pitches are in two groups with 12 hook-ups between them. One group with hardstanding close to the road has a distant view down a shallow valley to Melvich Bay beyond a low dune. The other has a grassy tent area with a similar view and further hard pitches without the sea in sight. Facilities are in an old building but are clean and functional. Meals are served all day at the busy inn, and the bar is popular, too.

NA	0.75	NP	22	16 AMP		

WC						MG	MB

Shop and beach 1 mile. Slipway 1.5 miles.

££££ M CL CS (i) WiFi

Directions: Halladale Inn is conspicuous in Melvich adjacent to A836, 1 mile west of its junction with A897.

GPS: N58°33.018' W003°54.775'
OS grid: 10 NC 888 640

All year

Craigdhu Camping and Caravan Site

Bettyhill, Sutherland, KW14 7SP
Tel: 01641 521273

The site's touring area is partly on a mown, level mound. From this high stance, some pitches look out over the wide sandy beach of Farr Bay 0.5 miles away. Other pitches, without the view but more shelter, are in a hollow. The facilities building is old and basic, but modern showers have full temperature and flow controls. 5 hook-ups are provided.

NA	1	NP	35			

WC						MG	MB

Slipway and beach 1 mile by road.

££££ M CL CS (i) WiFi

Directions: On A836 in Bettyhill, near the road's high point is a crossroads identified by petrol pumps, a post office and Bettyhill General Merchants. The site reception is at Dunbeadon House B&B at this crossroads. The site entrance is almost opposite. The asphalt road is steep in places.

GPS: N58°31.527' W004°13.283'
OS grid: 10 NC 707 619

April - September

Sealladh Na Mara *CL*

64 Clashaidy, Skerray, Thurso, Sutherland,
KW14 7TJ Tel: 01641 521210
www.caravanclub.co.uk

The *CL* is directly behind and above the rocky shore of Skerray Bay, looking across to small fishing boats moored to the sheltering pier. To the east is the contorted mass of contrasting rocks that is Coomb Island. To the north is the larger Eilean Nan Ron. The sheltered bay is valued by recreational boat owners, too, for this part of the coast is good for diving and sea angling. The hilly terrain is attractive to geologists and botanists, and signed paths link neighbouring crofting townships. Near the *CL* are pretty thatched cottages and a community shop selling genuinely local crafts and fairtrade produce.

| NA 0.5 | NP 5 | 0 AMP | | |

Pub 3 miles. Shop 8 miles.

££££ 🐕 ✝✝ Ⓜ CL CS ⓘ WiFi

Directions: Take A836 for 7-8 miles west from Bettyhill or east from Tongue. Turn north towards Skerray for 3.25 miles, passing a burial ground. Keep right all along the way, then turn left sp 'Skerray Harbour'. For the owner's house, turn right sp 'Clashaidy' (Clashaddy on the OS map), 0.25 miles before reaching the *CL*.

GPS: N58°32.477' W004°18.023'
OS grid: 10 NC 662 637

March - October

Bayview Caravan Site

Talmine, Lairg, Sutherland, IV27 4YS
Tel: 01847 601225

Beautiful views of the Rabbit Islands and part of extensive Tongue Bay can be enjoyed from this peaceful site at the head of Talmine Bay. The sandy beach revealed at low water rises to a shingle bank where it has become the tradition to build little beach henges. The pitches on this basic site are all fairly level and 4 have a gravelled surface. In a sturdy old building, the essential facilities are functional and supplied with hot water. The site is not regularly wardened, visitors being asked to call at the croft house on the road above. Owners of very long units should make advance arrangements, preferably by letter.

| NA 1 | NP 15 | 0 AMP | | |

Pub 1 mile.

££££ 🐕 ✝✝ Ⓜ CL CS ⓘ WiFi

Directions: From A838 at the western end of the Kyle of Tongue Causeway, turn right sp 'Talmine'. After 2.75 miles, take the right fork in the village at a small sp 'Campsite' down to the sea and the site.

GPS: N58°31.750' W004°25.918'
OS grid: 10 NC 585 626

April - September

Sango Sands Oasis Caravan and Camping Site 63

Durness, Sutherland, Highlands, IV27 4PZ
Tel: 01971 511726
www.sangosands.com

This is a large, well-kept, sprawling site and you are allowed to find any little nook and cranny to pitch on. You can even park on the cliff edge with a sheer drop to the sea below. The ground is partly level. Facilities include a campers' kitchen. The sandy bay is edged by rocky cliffs and the nearby islands make this bay ideal for snorkelling and body boarding. The beaches are a 1 min walk away, as is the tourist office's absorbing exhibition on the area's history, geology, botany, birds, crofting and fishing.

| NA | 10 | NP | 150 | 16 AMP | | |

| WC | | | | | | MG | MB |

Shop 200m.

££££ 🐕 ♦♦ Ⓜ CL CS ⓘ WiFi

Directions: Adjacent to A838 in Durness village overlooking Sango Bay.

GPS: N58°34.108' W004°44.603'
OS grid: 09 NC 405 678

April - October

Hamnavoe CL 64

Hamnavoe, Kinlochbervie, Lairg, Sutherland, IV27 4RR Tel: 01971 521045
www.caravanclub.co.uk

This idyllic site is perched high above narrow Loch Clash, with an unforgettable view to the west: if you are lucky, to the mountains of Harris. All around are the massive hills of Lewisian gneiss. A path direct from the CL leads down to the water. Individual level pitches on broken stone can be booked. It is extremely exposed, so the owner has thoughtfully provided 2 'storm refuge' pitches on the sheltered side of the bluff. Public showers are available at the marina in Kinlochbervie, which is one of Britain's busiest white fish landing ports.

| NA | 1 | NP | 5 | 16 AMP | | |

| WC | | | | | | MG | MB |

Shop and slipway 0.75 miles. Beach 2 miles.

££££ 🐕 ♦♦ Ⓜ CL CS ⓘ WiFi

Directions: From A838 at Rhiconich, take B801 to Kinlochbervie. Fork right uphill sp 'Oldshoremore' for 0.25 miles. The site is on the left past the hotel.

GPS: N58°27.728' W005°03.110'
OS grid: 9 NC 220 567

All year

Scourie
Caravan and Camping Park

Harbour Road, Scourie, Sutherland,
Highlands, IV27 4TG Tel: 01971 502060
www.scouriecampsitesutherland.com

This site provides a good view of the bay. The pitches are mostly terraced, some lawned and some on hardstandings. The site has excellent facilities, is well laid out, very tidy and close to the shops and the beach. Advance bookings are not taken. The water is exceptionally clear, making it ideal for snorkelling and diving. Golden eagles, deer, otters, badgers, wildcats and pine martens can be seen in the nearby hilly, walking country. Seals can also be seen locally.

| NA 4 | NP 75 | 10 AMP | | |

Slipway 200m.

£££££

Directions: Adjacent to A894 in Scourie, overlooking Scourie Bay. 26 miles from Durness and 45 miles from Ullapool.

GPS: N58°21.092' W005°09.319'
OS grid: 09 NC 154 447

April - September

Shore Caravan Site

106 Achmelvich, Lochinver, Sutherland,
Highlands, IV27 4JB Tel: 01571 844393
www.shorecaravansite.yolasite.com

The sea view from many of the pitches is to the point of land at Rubha Coigeach. Unseen from the site but immediately adjacent is a wide sandy beach. The seascape looks almost Mediterranean, and the silver sand in the bay and the flotilla of small craft all add to the ambience. This is an attractive site with plenty of space. The pitches are partly level, partly sloping with some hardstandings. No advanced bookings are taken: just turn up and relax. A provision shop and chip shop operate on site in the season.

| NA 6 | NP 60 | 6 AMP | | |

Pub and slipway 3.5 miles at Lochinver.

££££

Directions: From A837, 0.75 miles north of Lochinver, turn onto B869 sp 'Achmelvich'. In 1.5 miles, turn left sp 'Achmelvich' and follow road for a further 1.5 miles. In the village, go past the telephone box straight on to the site at the end of the road.

GPS: N58°10.135' W005°18.300'
OS grid: 15 NC 058 247

April - October

Clachtoll Beach Campsite

134 Clachtoll, Lochinver, Sutherland,
IV27 4JD Tel: 01571 855377
www.clachtollbeachcampsite.co.uk

From the pitches on this undulating dunes site, the view is generally westwards, taking in Rubha Reidh Lighthouse and the northern tip of Skye; also sometimes the mountains of Harris. The unmarked pitches on hard, well-drained sandy ground are mostly level and 24 have electricity. The number of regular visitors attests to the owner's hospitality and careful management. Towards the beach, displays in a ranger base explain the crofting tradition and local wildlife. In a former salmon bothy, an exhibition tells of the history and methods of coastal salmon netting.

NA	2.5	NP	40	16 AMP

Pub, shop and slipway 5 miles.

££££ 🐕 🚻 M CL CS (i) WiFi

Directions: From the north, the road is narrow, winding, sometimes steep with hairpins, exciting, and needs time and care. Leave A894 1.25 miles south of Unapool and take B869 for 18 miles to Clachtoll. Otherwise, leave A894 0.75 miles north of Lochinver and follow B869 for 5.5 easier miles to the site on the left.

GPS: N58°11.478' W005°20.010'
OS grid: 15 NC 040 273

Easter - September

Ardmair Point Holiday Park

Ardmair Point, Ullapool, Ross-shire,
IV26 2TN Tel: 07783 433040
www.ardmair.com

The 25 front row pitches above the pebble beach have a fine view to Isle Martin that masks the Summer Isles further out. Occupying a small peninsula with a curved pebble bay, this site is set amongst spectacular Highland scenery with the dramatic Ben Mhor Coigach mountain ridge as the backdrop for the sheltered sea loch. The more sheltered rear field has space for 50 tents. The shop on site has basic foods and snacks.

NA	8	NP	50	10 AMP

Pub 3 miles. Boat launching from site.

££££ 🐕 🚻 M CL CS (i) WiFi

Directions: 3 miles north of Ullapool adjacent to A835, look for the campsite sign by a telephone box.

GPS: N57°56.028' W005°11.781'
OS grid: 19 NH 109 983

April - September

Port A Bhaigh Campsite

Altandhu, Achiltibuie, Ullapool, Wester Ross,
IV26 2YR Tel: 01854 622339
www.portabhaigh.co.uk

Grassy terraces up the hillside give tents a grandstand view out to sea towards Harris and Lewis. Lower down, the hard pitches offer a similar view and many have electricity. All are level. The site was new in 2011 and the magnificent facilities building includes a small glazed seating area. Free WiFi is provided. Kayaks can be launched from the beach. Orcas, dolphins and porpoises can be seen close to shore. The adjacent village of Reiff is popular for rock climbing.

| NA 2.5 | NP 100 | 16 AMP | | |

Slipway 0.25 miles. Shop 1 mile.

££££ 🐕 ♦♦ M CL CS ⓘ WiFi

Directions: From A835 at Drumrunie (9.5 miles north of Ullapool), take the minor road along Lochs Lurgainn, Bad a' Ghaill and Osgaig for 11.5 miles. At the next junction, turn right sp 'Altandhu' and 'Reiff' and drive a further 2.75 miles. Turn left along the coast through Altandhu to the site entrance on the right. Reception is at Fuaran Bar opposite.

GPS: N58°03.233' W005°24.598'
OS grid: 15 NB 988 122

March - October

Broomfield Holiday Park

West Lane, Ullapool, Ross-shire, IV26 2UT
Tel: 01854 612020
www.broomfieldhp.com

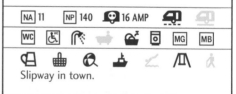

Right on the shore of Loch Broom, this site offers lovely views of the Summer Islands and the Hebrides. It is situated in an outstanding environment with wonderful scenery and amazing sunsets, but is conveniently located right next to Ullapool. There is still a major fishing fleet in Ullapool, so visitors can enjoy the comings and goings of the boats and the bounty that they bring home. All pitches are level and on two tiers, with 105 hook-ups. The beach is stony. The swimming pool and leisure centre are 0.5 miles away.

| NA 11 | NP 140 | 16 AMP | | |

Slipway in town.

£££ 🐕 ♦♦ M CL CS ⓘ WiFi

Directions: In Ullapool, follow the waterfront (Shore Street). Beyond the harbour, take the 2nd turning on the right (West Lane) where you will see the wide entrance to the site on the left.

GPS: N57°53.703' W005°09.750'
OS grid: 19 NH 125 938

Easter - September

Badrallach

Croft 9, Badrallach, Dundonnell,
Ross-shire, IV23 2QP
Tel: 01854 633281 www.badrallach.com

This small family-run site is situated in a beautiful and tranquil setting. The owners are romantic about the remoteness and still offer spring water and gas lights. The sea view is only partial once pitched, but is very fine from the shore or the road. There is no chemical disposal point or TV reception. There are 12 tent pitches and three caravan pitches on request.

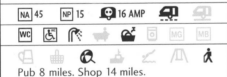

| NA 45 | NP 15 | 16 AMP | | |

| WC | | | | | MG | MB |

Pub 8 miles. Shop 14 miles.

££££ 🐕 †† M CL CS ⓘ WiFi

Directions: 12 miles south of Ullapool, turn off A835 at the Braemore Junction onto A832. After 11.5 miles, turn right sp 'Badralloch'. After a further 1.5 miles, turn right just after a small river bridge sp 'Badralloch'. Follow the single-track road for a further 5.5 miles and the site is on the left.

Scottish TOURIST BOARD ★★★★ CAMPING PARK

GPS: N57°52.411' W005°15.571'
OS grid: 19 NH 066 915

All Year

Northern Lights

Croft 9, Badcaul, Dundonnell,
Ross-shire, IV23 2QY
Tel: 07786 274175 / 01697 371379

The outlook from here across Little Loch Broom is dramatised by Deinn Ghoblach opposite. This wonderful little site with some hardstandings is kept neat and tidy and well mown. There is room for 12 touring caravans, motorhomes or tents. The facilities are housed in a sympathetically refurbished old stone building. Access to sandy beaches is about 4 miles away. TV reception is very poor because the site is surrounded by hills which make for a dramatic sea and landscape.

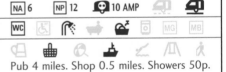

| NA 6 | NP 12 | 10 AMP | | |

| WC | | | | | MG | MB |

Pub 4 miles. Shop 0.5 miles. Showers 50p.

££££ 🐕 †† M CL CS ⓘ WiFi

Directions: 12 miles south of Ullapool, turn off A835 at A832. Follow sp 'Dundonnell', 'Aultbea' and 'Gairloch' for approximately 18 miles. You will pass the Dundonnell Hotel and the site is 4.75 miles past the hotel on the right.

GPS: N57°52.060' W005°20.078'
OS grid: 19 NH 024 914

April - September

Gruinard Bay Caravan Park

Laide, Wester Ross, Highlands, IV22 2ND
Tel: 01445 731225
www.gruinardbay.co.uk

The site's sea view is out to the Summer Isles and Gruinard Island with a backdrop of the sweep of the Assynt. The small, well-cared-for, family-run park is beside the sandy beach in the village of Laide. All the pitches are level and 18 have electricity. The ruins of the Chapel of Sand are adjacent to the park and, along with the uninterrupted sea views, add real atmosphere to the setting. You can walk 2 miles down a track from Laide to the ruins of Slaggan, where there is also a superb beach.

| NA 3.5 | NP 35 | 10 AMP | | |

| WC | | | | | MG | MB |

Pub 0.25 miles. Slipway 1 mile.

£££ 🐕 †† M CL CS (i) WiFi

Directions: 12 miles south of Ullapool, turn off A835 at Braemore Junction. Follow sp 'Dundonnell', 'Aultbea' and 'Gairloch' for approximately 29 miles. The site is on the right between the villages of Sand and Laide.

GPS: N57°51.997' W005°32.193'
OS grid: 19 NG 903 918

April - October

Inverewe Gardens Camping and Caravanning Club Site

Poolewe, Achnasheen, Wester Ross,
IV22 2LF Tel: 01445 781249
www.campingandcaravanningclub.co.uk

The wide spacing of the level pitches allows most a view to the inner reach of Loch Ewe, over which the sun can set spectacularly. To see more, drive or ride along B8057 on the western side of the loch to Cove. On the near and far shores are numerous remains from operations that supported naval action in WWII and especially the Russian Arctic convoys. A small exhibition in Poolewe is a forerunner of a planned museum covering those until now secret activities. This is one of the prettiest club sites we know, with its spacious emerald lawns, scattered trees, natural boulders, and bright little flower gardens.

| NA 2 | NP 55 | 16 AMP | | |

| WC | | | | | MG | MB |

Sandy beach 3 miles.

£££ 🐕 †† M CL CS (i) WiFi

Directions: The site is adjacent to A832 in Poolewe between the river bridge and Inverewe Gardens.

GPS: N57°46.073' W005°35.953'
OS grid: 19 NG 861 811

April - October

Gairloch Caravan and Camping Holiday Park

Mihol Road, Strath, Gairloch, Wester Ross, IV21 2BX Tel: 01445 712373
www.gairlochcaravanpark.com

The park looks out to the Isle of Skye and west to the Outer Hebrides. Across the loch lie the mountains of the Torridon Forest, creating a magnificent landscape. All sorts of amenities are right on the doorstep, the sea is just across the road, and it is only 0.5 miles to a sandy beach. In this neat, well-maintained site, all pitches are level, half have electricity, and 12 are hard. 2 static caravans and a cottage are for hire. Visits to Rubha Reidh Lighthouse and boat trips to the Shiant Islands are popular.

NA	10	NP	75	16 AMP		
WC					MG	MB

Shop adjacent. Slipway 2 miles.

££££ 🐕 †† M CL CS ⓘ WiFi

Directions: Turn west off A832 in Gairloch onto B8021. After 0.5 miles, turn right immediately after the Millcroft Hotel. The site is on your right.

GPS: N57°43.895' W005°42.165'
OS grid: 19 NG 797 774

April - October

Sands Caravan and Camping Park

Gairloch, Wester Ross, IV21 2DL
Tel: 01445 712152
www.sandscaravanandcamping.co.uk

From the higher pitches, the view extends over Loch Gairloch and Longa Island to Rona and Skye. Pitches lower down, without the view, are sheltered by the dunes. The beach is long and sandy. All pitches are firm and well drained, and 18 are hard surfaced. About two thirds are level and half have electricity. The very large site is tidy and well run, and includes a games room and a substantial shop.

NA	55	NP	250	16 AMP		
WC					MG	MB

Pub 2 miles.

££££ 🐕 †† M CL CS ⓘ WiFi

Directions: Turn west off A832 in Gairloch, take B8021 towards Melvaig for 3.5 miles to the site.

GPS: N57°44.438' W005°45.862'
OS grid: 19 NG 758 784

April - October

Shieldaig Camping Area

Shieldaig Village, Ross-shire, IV54 8XW

This is a village grazing area where camping is permitted. It is a beautiful spot and the exceptional environment should be well respected. There are superb views over Lochs Shieldaig and Torridon and to Lewis and Harris in the far distance, often with beautiful sunsets. The site being unsupervised and unserviced except for a water tap, campers are trusted to donate about £5 in the honesty box. Public toilets and shops can be found a few mins walk away in the village.

NA	0.5	NP	20	🕑 0 AMP		
WC					MG	MB

Slipway in village.

£££ CL CS WiFi

Directions: The site is situated in Shieldaig village off A896 between Lochcarron and Kinlochewe. From the south, leave A896 at the 2nd sp for the village. The site is on the left in 0.25 miles.

GPS: N57°31.530' W005°38.888'
OS grid: 24 NG 816 541

April - October

Applecross Campsite

Applecross, Strathcarron, Wester Ross, IV54 8ND Tel: 01520 744268
www.applecross-campsite.co.uk

The sea view across the Inner Sound to Raasay and the mountains of Skye is limited by the sheltering boundary trees. The journey in is spectacular, whether it is along the meandering coastal route with sweeping panoramas of Loch Torridon then the Western Isles and Rona, or over the mountains by the long, sometimes challenging climb and descent. The high standards of the meals and the growing popularity of the camping pods are just two factors contributing to a well-liked site. The pitches are mostly level, 10 are hard, and 15 have electricity.

NA	6	NP	60	🕑 16 AMP		
WC					MG	MB

Shop 0.5 miles.

£££ CL CS WiFi

Directions: From 1 mile south of Shieldaig, take the coastal scenic route sp 'Applecross'. Alternatively, from 7.5 miles further south, also turn right for Applecross and enjoy the challenge.

GPS: N57°25.901' W005°48.696'
OS grid: 24 NG 712 443

Easter - October

The Wee Campsite

Dunrovin, Croft Road, Lochcarron,
Ross-shire, IV54 8YA
Tel: 07876 642355

The middle reach of Loch Carron can be seen well from the upper two tent terraces and one hardstanding terrace of this small, well-sheltered, quiet site with hospitable owners. Facilities are simple and homely, but unfortunaltely without chemical disposal. All pitches are level, 6 are hard and have electricity. A few mins walk away, attractive Lochcarron village has a laundry.

* Temporarily closed due to illness as of February 2014. Check in advance.

| NA | 0.5 | NP | 21 | 16 AMP | | |

| WC | | | | MG | MB |

Pub, shop and slipway 1 mile.

££££

Directions: From the south on A87 towards Kyle of Lochalsh, turn right onto A890 at Auchtertyre. Continue round the head of Loch Carron to a T-junction. Turn left onto A896 to Lochcarron village. At Lochcarron Garage, turn right up Croft Road to the clearly sp site on the right.

GPS: N57°24.140' W005°29.163'
OS grid: 25 NG 906 401

Easter - October

Ardelve Caravan and Camping Park

Ardelve, Dornie, Kyle, Wester Ross,
IV40 8DY Tel: 01599 555231
www.ardelvecaravanandcampingpark.co.uk

The slightly sloping site gives all pitches a view across the junction of Loch Alsh and Loch Duich to the mountains of Glenshiel. Much photographed Eilean Donan is in the foreground and can be visited. Quietly situated right beside the water, the site has 16 level, hard pitches with electricity on two terraces. The large space for tents slopes gradually. Two small toilet blocks are modest and clean. With no reception on site, the owner attends in the evening. Bookings are not taken.

| NA | 2 | NP | 16 | | | |

| WC | | | | MG | MB |

££££

Directions: The village of Ardelve is adjacent to A87, 8 miles east of Kyle of Lochalsh and 2.5 miles east of the A890 junction. Travelling from the east takes you past Shiel Bridge, Eilean Donan Castle and the Loch Long Bridge. Ardelve is just over the bridge from Dornie. Turn off sp 'Ardelve' with the campsite symbol.

GPS: N57°16.932' W005°31.556'
OS grid: 33 NG 875 267

Easter - October

Camus More Campsite

Camus More, Kilmuir, Isle of Skye,
IV51 9YS
Tel: 01470 552312

Uig Bay
Caravan and Campsite

10 Idrigill, Uig, Isle of Skye, IV51 9XU
Tel: 01470 542714
www.uig-camping-skye.co.uk

This is a gem of unsurpassed tranquillity, set at the top of a bank behind a rocky, pebbly beach. The wide panorama of the Minch includes the skyline silhouette of Harris over which the sun sets. The remote restfulness of the place is preserved by its distance from supplies and the very modest facilities of a toilet, washbasin, shower and 2 deep sinks. Tents pitch on the mown grass of old lazybeds. A motorhome or 2 would be welcomed but not a convoy. A hilarious half hour could be spent in Macmurdie's Exhibition of local heritage and things quirky.

The site lies right beside Uig Bay. 2 privileged pitches are close by the waterfront and stony beach. The remainder of the site stretches inland, with first the hardstandings then smooth, firm, slightly sloping grass. All have fragmented or wider views of the bay. A couple of hundred yards away are the ferry terminal, fuel, shops, pottery and a brewery. Within easy reach are miles of the celebrated Trotternish cliffs and crofting coastal landscapes, spectacular rock features on the east coast, and memorials and museums recording key events and people.

NA 1   NP 8   0 AMP

Pub, shop and slipway 6 miles in Uig.

NA 2.5   NP 30   16 AMP

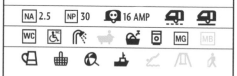

££££ 🐕 †† M CL ·CS ⓘ WiFi

££££ 🐕 †† ·M· CL CS ⓘ WiFi

Directions: From Uig, take A855 north for 5.25 miles towards Kilmuir. Turn left sp 'Camus More' and, after 1 mile, turn left at the crossroads through a gate. The site is on the right in 0.25 miles.

Directions: At the base of the ferry pier in Uig, take the road sp 'Uig Caravan and Campsite' for 180m to the site.

GPS: N57°39.017' W006°24.250'
OS grid: 23 NG 373 708

GPS: N57°35.133' W006°22.767'
OS grid: 23 NG 381 637

May - September

All year

Am Bothan Bunkhouse

Ferry Road, Leverburgh, Isle of Harris,
HS5 3UA Tel: 01859 520251
www.ambothan.com

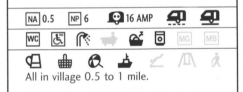

On high ground behind Leverburgh, the bunkhouse and parking area overlook the village, ferry terminal, harbour area, and the Sound of Harris. The bunkhouse, with 3 hardstandings in front for motorhomes and grassy space behind for 3 tents, is a handy stopping point for the ferry to Berneray and North Uist. The ablutions, cooking and dishwashing facilities are open to campers. The lounge is a social centre which frequently holds musical evenings and has a wide spectrum of guests with whom to exchange experiences.

| NA 0.5 | NP 6 | 16 AMP | | |

All in village 0.5 to 1 mile.

£££ CL CS WiFi

Directions: From the ferry terminal at Leverburgh, follow sp 'Am Bothan'. The red bunkhouse is at the top of a slight hill.

GPS: N57°46.061' W007°01.133'
OS grid: 18 NG 016 863

All year

Lickisto Blackhouse Camping

1 Lickisto, Isle of Harris, HS3 3EL
Tel: 01859 530485
www.freewebs.com/vanvon

The sea view is down the slender length of Loch Stockinish that is good for kayaking and where otters play and porpoises may be seen. In the rocky remoteness of South Harris, this site is a lush oasis. 3 pitches with electricity for motorhomes have a high vantage point. Tent pitches have their own dispersed bays among the heather, irises and willows. The shells of blackhouses that have stood for 2 centuries hold modern ablutions and a traditional, cosy lounge for social gatherings. Yurts complete the accommodation. Hosts John and Harvey offer a warm welcome, fresh bread and eggs. Note that there is no chemical disposal here.

| NA 9 | NP 3 | 16 AMP | | |

Pub and shop 7 miles at Tarbert.

£££ CL CS WiFi

Directions: From Tarbert, take A859 south for 4.5 miles. Turn left along a twisting but well-surfaced road for a further 2.75 miles to the site, which is well sp at junctions.

GPS: N57°49.683' W006°51.267'
OS grid: 14 NG 120 923

April - October

Minch View Touring Campsite

10 Drinishader, Isle of Harris, HS3 3DX
Tel: 01859 511207
www.minchview.wordpress.com

The small croft site has a view past several small islands to East Loch Tarbert along which ferries pass from Tarbert to Uig and Lochmaddy. 10 almost level, grass pitches for tents are on former lazy beds. The level, hard space can accommodate 5 motorhomes or 4 caravans. How many of either is at the discretion of the owner. A modest, modern outbuilding holds 2 spotlessly clean, simple toilets, a shower and a laundry cum washing-up room, all with modern equipment. From site you can walk a circuit around Loch Plocrapool on footpaths and quiet roads giving you the chance to take in the spectacular landscape.

| NA 0.5 | NP 14 | | | |

Pub 5 miles. Shop and slipway 0.5 miles.

££££ 🐕 †† M CL CS (i) WiFi

Directions: From Tarbert, take A859 south for 2.5 miles. Turn left sp 'Miabhag' and 'Drinisiader'. The site is sp on the left opposite a loch 0.5 miles further on.

GPS: N57°50.750' W006°45.583'
OS grid: 14 NG 176 939

April - September

Traigh na Beirigh (Berrie Beach) Campsite

15 Cnip, Maibhaig, Uig, Isle of Lewis, HS2 9HS
Tel: 01851 672265

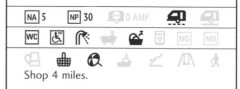

As you approach you overlook the site which lies in dunes beside a mile-long crescent of brilliant silver sand, giving a view to islands and headlands. Level places can be found in hollows and atop the mounds. Seasonals occupy many of the best spots. 30 caravans or motorhomes can be accommodated and an unspecified number of tents. Washrooms are well built and clean, with showers costing £1. Fuel is available at the shop towards Timsgarry.

| NA 5 | NP 30 | 0 AMP | | |

Shop 4 miles.

££££ 🐕 †† M CL CS (i) WiFi

Directions: From Stornoway, take A859 south, then A858 west. Continue west onto B8011, then north. 1.5 miles beyond Cairisiadar, turn right over bridge and go through the villages of Cliff, Bhaltos (Valtos), and Cnip (Kneep). The site is conspicuous on approach.

GPS: N58°12.972' W006°56.433'
OS grid: 13 NB 100 359

May - October

Horgabost Campsite

Horgabost, Isle of Harris, HS3 3HR
Tel: 01859 550386

The site has a natural, unspoiled setting on dunes looking down onto a wide, silver sand beach and the Atlantic. Pitching is on hard, well-drained turf. Inside the unprepossessing steel containers are immaculately cleaned facilities comprising thoroughly modern equipment and finishes. Note that the nearest chemical disposal point is at Leverburgh. A small shop operates in summer and a mobile shop calls. A bus stop is located at the entrance. Arts, crafts, tweeds and archaeological excavations are local features. Day visits to St Kilda from Leverburgh are popular.

| NA 5 | NP 80 | 0 AMP | | |

Pub, shop and slipway 7 miles at Leverburgh.

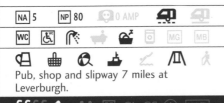

Directions: The site is on the southwest coast of Harris adjacent to A859 opposite the Isle of Taransay. The site is clearly visible beside the sands on approach from east or south and is sp. Instead of a reception building, registration information is posted at the entrance. Bookings are not taken but nobody needs to be turned away.

GPS: N57°51.717' W006°58.633'
OS grid: 18 NG 048 967

May - September

Balranald Hebridean Holidays

Hougharry, North Uist, HS6 5DL
Tel: 01876 510304
www.balranaldhebrideanholidays.com

Walk 18m from the site gate up to the dune crest and before you is a vista that you will not easily forget. An area of dazzling silver sand rings a wide bay framed by headlands. Near the horizon are the distinctively shaped Monach Isles. Dipping below the horizon at 50 miles is St Kilda. Newly opened in 2012, this level site lies in the RSPB Balranald Nature Reserve with its colourful carpet of the flowering machair in summer. The rare corncrake can be seen and its distinctive clock-winding call heard from the site. 10 hard pitches for caravans have electricity.

| NA 2 | NP 20 | 16 AMP | | |

Pub 3 miles. Shop 2 miles. Slipway 5 miles.

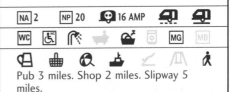

Directions: The site is at the extreme western point of A865. Turn off A865 sp 'Balranald Nature Reserve'. After 0.75 miles, fork left sp 'Toilets' and continue to the site.

GPS: N57°36.327' W007°31.125'
OS grid: 18 NF 705 705

April - September

Kilbride Campsite

9 West Kilbride, Lochboisdale, South Uist,
HS8 5TT Tel: 01878 700568
www.kilbridecampsite.co.uk

The site is immediately across the coast road from a small sandy bay set into the rocky shoreline. The view extends to the islands of Lingay, Fuday, Eriskay and the northern tip of Barra. Completely new in 2012, the unsheltered site has a fine facilities block built to the latest standards. The 20 hard pitches have electricity as do 7 of the grass pitches for tents. In the adjacent walled garden, an attractive little showroom sells local knitting, other crafts, and produce from the garden. The area has significant history and heritage, and abundant wildlife.

NA 2	NP 30	16 AMP		
WC				MG MB

Pub and slipway 0.5 miles. Shop 2 miles.

£££ WiFi

Directions: From Lochboisdale ferry terminal, follow A865 north. At Dalibrugh (Dalabrog), turn south onto D888 near the Borrodale Hotel and follow the road for 4.5 miles. Turn left sp 'Sound of Barra Ferry'. The site is in Kilbride (Cille Bhrighde) on the left in 0.25 miles.

Scottish
TOURIST BOARD
★★★★
CAMPING PARK

GPS: N57°06.200' W007°21.367'
OS grid: 31 NF 757 142

Easter - September

Croft No. 2 Campsite

Scurrival Points, Eoligarry, Isle of Barra,
HS9 5YD Tel: 01871 890327
www.barracamping.com

Photo courtesy of Angus MacLeod

In a slight hollow, with some shelter from most directions, the somewhat sloping grass site has a view past the islands of Fuday and Lingay to South Uist. Facilities are limited to water, chemical disposal and electricity. Public toilets are 0.5 miles away, but some tent campers bring their own toilet. The fields are carpeted with primroses in spring and hold many of Barra's hundreds of wildflower species. Nearby, you can watch planes operating the only scheduled services in the world from a shell sand beach at low tide. The site owners are notably welcoming and helpful.

NA 1	NP 5	10/16 AMP		
WC				MG MB

Pub and slipway 5 miles at Northbay.

££ WiFi

Directions: From the northeasterly extreme of A888, turn north towards the airport and the terminal for the ferry to Eriskay (Eirisgeidh). Continue on this road almost to its very end at the northern tip of Barra. Croft 2 is the last house but one on this road.

GPS: N57°03.317' W007°26.683'
OS grid: 31 NF 700 092

April - October

## Borve ## Camping and Caravan Site	91

104A Borve, Isle of Barra, HS9 5XR
Tel: 01871 810878
www.barracamping.co.uk

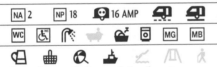

The site is directly behind a west-facing inlet surrounded by part of the hamlet of Borve. The uninterrupted view from all the pitches is out over the open Atlantic. On a level, firm, well-drained shelf above the beach, the new site, opened in 2012, is sheltered from the south by a bank that carries the coast road. The pitches, all with electricity, are distributed between two groups, one each side of the facilities building that includes a kitchen and laundry. The cove would be a good base from which to launch kayaks.

NA 2	NP 18	16 AMP		
WC				

Pub, shop and slipway 2.5 miles at Castlebay.

££££ 🐕 †† M CL CS (i) WiFi

Directions: From Castlebay, take A888 west then north for 2.5 miles to the site on the left of and below the road.

GPS: N56°58.733' W007°30.883'
OS grid: 31 NF 652 011

April - October

## Barra Holidays @Croft183	92

Croft 183, Bolnabodach, Isle of Barra,
HS9 5UT Tel: 01871 890373
www.croft183.com

The site is in a traditional crofting village, the descendant of a shore-side fishing community dating from 2000 BC. In the small, family-owned campsite, 4 of the widely spaced, elevated pitches have a view across the eastern approaches to Castle Bay. In addition to new toilet facilities, the genial hosts have provided a kitchen with microwave cooker and meal table, and abundant information on local history, wildlife and public transport. Castlebay has a leisure centre, heritage museum, Kisimul Castle and boat trips to Mingulay.

NA 1	NP 6	16 AMP		
WC				

Pub and slipway 2 miles. Shop 4 miles.

££££ 🐕 †† M CL CS (i) WiFi

Directions: From Castlebay ferry terminal, turn right onto A888 for 4.25 miles. The site is clearly sp on the left at the brow of a hill.

GPS: N56°59.119' W007°24.633'
OS grid: 31 NF 714 012

April - October

Moorcroft Holidays

17 Carinish, North Uist, HS6 5HN
Tel: 01876 580305
www.moorcroftholidays.co.uk

The view from all pitches is across the islet-strewn lagoon of Oitir Mhor. This site could be considered to be the highest grade of the sites in the Western Isles. The 10 level, hard caravan pitches all have electricity. Tents are on grass, with some areas level. Facilities are, in a word, palatial and include a kitchen for campers. Walks can be taken on both the seaward and landward sides of the site.

| NA | 1.5 | NP | 30 | 16 AMP | | |

| WC | | | | | | MG | MB |

Pub 1 mile. Shop 3 miles. Slipway 4 miles.

£££ M CL CS WiFi

Directions: From South Uist, take A865 to the northernmost point on Benbecula. Continue on A865 for 3.25 miles, crossing causeways and the island of Grimsay. The site is sp on the left.

GPS: N57°31.133' W007°17.167'
OS grid: 22 NF 836 597

April - September

Skye Camping and Caravanning Club Site

Borve, Arnisort, Edinbane, Portree,
Isle of Skye, IV51 9PS Tel: 01470 582230
www.skyecamp.com

This franchised club site stands on the shore of Loch Greshornish. The land rises away from the rocky beach and is partly terraced, giving almost all pitches a good view of the water. Some level pitches are hard, some on grass. Ultra-modern facilities include a dog-wash bay. Formaldehyde-based toilet chemicals cannot be emptied. The shop at reception has basic foods including eggs from the owners' croft. In a stone barn are a campers' kitchen and a supreme information display. Minibus tours start from the site and service buses pass the gate. Dunvegan Castle is too near to be missed.

| NA | 7 | NP | 105 | 16 AMP | | |

| WC | | | | | | MG | MB |

Pub 1 mile. Shop on site and 2 miles.

£££ M CL CS WiFi

Directions: From Portree, take A87, then A850 northwest for 12.5 miles almost to Edinbane. The site is visible below the road and the entrance is marked by conspicuous flags.

GPS: N57°29.144' W006°25.814'
OS grid: 23 NG 344 525

March - October

Kinloch Campsite

Millburn, Dunvegan, Isle of Skye, IV55 8GU
Tel: 01470 521210
www.kinloch-campsite.co.uk

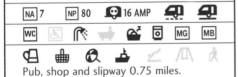

At the head of Loch Dunvegan and near the village of Dunvegan, all the site's pitches overlook the loch. Continuing development is increasing the number of hard, level pitches with electricity. Lightweight boats can be launched from a clear track on the stony beach. Dunvegan Castle and gardens comprise the most significant historical venue for miles around. Look out for the little museum in the village.

| NA 7 | NP 80 | 16 AMP | | |

Pub, shop and slipway 0.75 miles.

£££ £

Directions: From Broadford, take A87 for 16 miles to Sligachan, then A863 for 22.5 miles almost to Dunvegan. In Kilmuir, turn left sp 'Glendale' with campsite symbol to the site.

GPS: N57°25.894' W006°34.681'
OS grid: 23 NG 253 472

April - October

Glenbrittle Campsite

Glenbrittle, Isle of Skye, IV47 8TA
Tel: 01478 640404
www.dunvegancastle.com

Lying in an arc of dune land behind the extensive sandy beach are grass pitches on different levels. Small bays and alleys are mown, providing shelter in the hollows for tents and higher vantage points for motorhomes. Many look out across wide Loch Brittle to Canna and low-lying Sanday, with Rum towering above a headland. 8 hard, level pitches have electricity for motorhomes. A shop combined with reception stocks a range of non-perishable and frozen foods, also camping equipment, guides and maps. Of several paths, one leads into the nearest corrie of the Cuillin Mountains, which dominate the site.

| NA 10 | NP 220 | 16 AMP | | |

£££ £

Directions: From Broadford, take A87 for 16 miles to Sligachan, then A863 for 5.25 miles. Turn left onto B8009 for 2 miles, then left onto a single-track road sp 'Glenbrittle'. Follow to the site at the end of the road.

GPS: N57°12.167' W006°17.483'
OS grid: 32 NG 413 206

April - September

Camusdarach Campsite

Camusdarach, Arisaig, Inverness-shire,
PH39 4NT Tel: 01687 450221
www.camusdarach.com

Managed in an environmentally responsible manner and with absolutely pristine facilities, this lovely site has only partial sea views from some pitches, half of which have electricity. The grounds are very well cared for and large mature trees provide excellent shelter. A footpath from the site gives access to the superb sandy beaches, which are a mere 3 mins stroll away. The beach is also licensed for weddings! There is a café and functions open to the public are held.

| NA 3 | NP 42 | 16 AMP | | |

Pub 3 miles. Shop and slipway 4 miles.

£££ 🐕 ♟ M CL CS ⓘ WiFi

Directions: From A830 Fort William-Mallag road, turn left onto B8008 at Arisaig. The site is sp in approximately 4 miles on the left.

GPS: N56°57.262' W005°50.782'
OS grid: 40 NM 662 916

March - October

Traigh CL

Tigh-Na-Bruaich, Arisaig, Inverness-shire,
PH39 4NT Tel: 01687 450645
www.caravanclub.co.uk

Everyone gets a beautiful sea view from this very slightly sloping Caravan Club CL on short grass over firm sand. The sandy beach is only a few metres away. The site has an easy entrance and is immediately next door to Silversands Caravan Site 99 .

| NA 1 | NP 5 | 0 AMP | | |

Pub 2 miles. Shop and slipway 2.5 miles.

££££ 🐕 ♟ M CL CS ⓘ WiFi

Directions: From A830 Fort William-Mallag road, turn left onto B8008 at Arisaig. The site is on the left in 2.5 miles.

GPS: N56°56.362' W005°51.480'
OS grid: 40 NM 654 898

All Year

Silversands Caravan Site

Portnaluchaig, Arisaig, Inverness-shire, PH39 4NT
Tel: 01687 450269

Nicely mown and level, this is a lovely little site but the facilities are basic. Pitches are distributed in little nooks and crannies all over the site, providing seclusion for those who want it. Access to the sandy beach, rock pools and sea is only a short walk away. Campers really love this site, and it can be very busy at weekends.

| NA 10 | NP 18 | 10 AMP | | |
| WC | | | | MG | MB |

Pub 2 miles. Shop and slipway 2.5 miles.

££££ 🐕 ♗♙ M CL CS ⓘ WiFi

Directions: From A830 Fort William-Mallaig road, turn left onto B8008 at Arisaig. The site is on the left in 2.5 miles, next to the Caravan Club CL 98.

GPS: N56°56.362' W005°51.480'
OS grid: 40 NM 653 898

March - October

Sunnyside Croft Touring Caravan and Camping Site

2 Bunacaimbe, Arisaig, Inverness-shire, PH39 4NT Tel: 01687 450643
www.sunnysidetouringsite.co.uk

Photo courtesy of Ian Reid

Set back 200m from the shore on rising ground, this site has views across the water to the Small Isles. A path leads directly to the sandy beach. The meticulously planned building houses reception with a small shop, a covered seating area, microwave and ice-pack freezer for tenters, family bathroom and disabled unit in addition to the usual ablutions. All pitches have electricity. Environmental care is prominent. Meat from the croft's livestock may be on sale in the shop. Ranger-led walks are available.

| NA 2 | NP 40 | 16 AMP | | |
| WC | | | | MG | MB |

Pub 0.75 miles. Shops and slipway 2 miles.

£££ 🐕 ♗♙ M CL CS ⓘ WiFi

Directions: On A830 Fort William-Mallaig road, turn left onto B8008 at Arisaig. The site is clearly sp on the left in 2 miles.

GPS: N56°55.950' W005°51.750'
OS grid: 40 NM 651 889

All year

Portnadoran Caravan Site

Arisaig, Inverness-shire,
PH39 4NT Tel: 01687 450267
www.arisaigcampsite.co.uk

Photo courtesy of Audrey MacDonald

The site is right on the edge of a soft, white sandy beach interspersed with rocks. There are stunning views as the entire site overlooks the Isles of Skye, Eigg, Rum and Muck. It is a wonderful, informally managed, commercial site with hook-ups for two thirds of the pitches. People return year after year. Porpoises and otters are seen locally and kids will love the rock pooling. Small boats can be launched from the site.

NA 4   NP 40   16 AMP

WC   MG   MB

Pub 0.5 miles. Shop and slipway 2 miles. Showers 20p.

££££   M   CL CS   (i)   WiFi

Directions: From A830 Fort William-Mallag road, turn left onto B8008 at Arisaig. The site is sp on the left in approximately 2 miles.

GPS: N56°55.978' W005°51.653'
OS grid: 40 NM 650 891

April - October

Invercaimbe
Caravan and Camping Site

Arisaig, Inverness-shire, PH39 4NT
Tel: 01687 450375

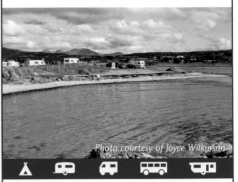

Photo courtesy of Joyce Wilkinson

This small, family-run site is situated on the shoreline with all pitches overlooking the islands of Eigg, Rum, Muck and Skye. The ground is mostly uneven, so before booking it is best to check that a suitable pitch is available. All have electricity. The sandy beach is safe for play and swimming, and mountains form a fine backdrop to the site. Boat trips can be taken to all the Inner Hebridean islands. Book early for summer holidays.

NA 2   NP 18   16 AMP

WC   MG   MB

Pub 0.5 miles. Shop and slipway 2 miles.

£££   M   CL CS   (i)   WiFi

Directions: From A830 Fort William-Mallaig road, turn left onto B8008 at Arisaig. The site is sp on the left in about 1 mile.

GPS: N56°55.638' W005°51.552'
OS grid: 40 NM 652 883

mid March - mid October

The Croft "Back of Keppoch" [103]

"Back of Keppoch", Arisaig, Inverness-shire, PH39 4NS
Tel: 01687 450200

Photo courtesy of Marion Macmillan

This is a slightly sloping site with basic facilities. However, it is in a wonderful part of the world, in an interesting sandy and rocky bay. The views are very beautiful and, being west facing, there could be spectacular sunsets. There is direct access to the sandy beach and its rocky outcrops and rock pools.

| NA | 3 | NP | 15 | 10 AMP | | |

| WC | | | | | | MG | MB |

Pub 0.5 miles. Shop and slipway 2 miles.

££££ M CL CS (i) WiFi

Directions: From A830 Fort William-Mallag road, turn left onto B8008 at Arisaig. Turn left sp 'Back of Keppoch' and follow the road for 0.5 miles. The site entrance is sp on the right.

GPS: N56°55.417' W005°52.090'
OS grid: 40 NM 647 880

Gorten Sands Caravan Site [104]

Gorten Sands Farm, Arisaig, Inverness-shire, PH39 4NS
Tel: 01687 450283

Next to a white sandy beach, this is a very small and pleasant site with good facilities and wonderful views. Half of the pitches have hook-up. The shoreline is rocky and should make for interesting snorkelling and fishing. The campsite is part of the Macdonald family working hill and coastal farm, where traditional harvesting methods are still employed.

| NA | 6 | NP | 45 | 6 AMP | | |

| WC | | | | | | MG | MB |

Pub 0.75 miles. Shop and slipway 2 miles. Small boats launched on site.

££££ M CL CS (i) WiFi

Directions: From A830 Fort William-Mallaig road, turn left onto B8008 at Arisaig. Turn left sp 'Back of Keppoch' and follow the road for approximately 1 mile to the end, where you will find the site entrance.

GPS: N56°55.283' W005°52.730'
OS grid: 40 NM 640 878

May - September

Resipole Holiday Park

Loch Sunart, Acharacle, Argyll, PH36 4HX
Tel: 01967 431235
www.resipole.co.uk

Photo courtesy of Resipole Holiday Park

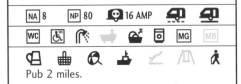

The pitches on this site offer views directly across Loch Sunart to the hills and wooded shore beyond. The site is immaculate, spacious and level with well kept lawns and electricity for half the pitches. Nearby is part of the Ancient Caledonian Oak Forest where you can spot red deer and a variety of birdlife. Garbh Eilean wildlife hide sits 2 miles east on a rocky knoll on the shore of the loch overlooking two small islands where seals and otters can be seen. From the hide, a patient wildlife enthusiast might even catch a glimpse of a golden eagle.

| NA 8 | NP 80 | 16 AMP | | |

| WC | | | | | | MG | MB |

Pub 2 miles.

£££

Directions: From the south on A82, from Oban on A828, or from Fort William, cross on the Corran Ferry to Ardgour. Take A861 21 miles past Strontian to the site on the right of the road at Resipole.

GPS: N56°42.650' W005°43.200'
OS grid: 40 NM 724 639

Easter or April - October

Far View Campsite

Pier Road, Kilchoan, Ardnamurchan, Argyll, PH36 4LH Tel: 01972 510346
www.farviewcottage.co.uk

Photo courtesy of Julie Allcock

This little site has a garden-like feel and is terraced into the slope to give each pitch a view across the entrance to the Sound of Mull towards Tobermory. Each pitch has electricity, is gravelled and is almost level. Useful details such as footpaths and guided wildlife walks are displayed outside reception. The nearby community hall includes a tourist office, showers and a café. Wildlife cruises run from the Kilchoan ferry slipway 0.4 miles away. Nearby is Ardnamurchan Point, the most westerly point on the British mainland.

| NA 1 | NP 5 | 16 AMP | | |

| WC | | | | | | MG | MB |

Pub and shop 0.5 miles. Slipway 0.25 miles. Beach 5 miles.

££££

Directions: From Fort William, take A830 to Lochailort, then A861 to Salen and B8007 to Kilchoan. The site is at Far Cottage, 0.4 miles before the ferry slip.

GPS: N56°41.650' W006°05.767'
OS grid: 47 NM 493 633

All year

Bunree Caravan Club Site

Onich, Fort William, PH33 6SE
Tel: 01855 821283
www.caravanclub.co.uk

This well managed site is located on the stony shore of Loch Linnhe. All pitches have sea and mountain views and electricity, and mature trees give the site a wonderful natural feel. Reception has a few essentials for sale and there is a small games room on site. The bus to Fort William stops 300m from the site. Non-members are welcome.

| NA 7 | NP 99 | 16 AMP | | |

Shop 1.5 miles. Forest walks 0.25 miles.

£££ CL CS WiFi

Directions: From the south on A82 from Loch Lomond or A828 from Oban, cross Ballachulish Bridge. 1 mile past Onich, cross a small river and turn 1st left at the Caravan Club sign. Follow a narrow road with traffic lights to the site.

GPS: N56°42.925' W005°13.750'
OS grid: 41 NN 021 626

March - January

Seaview Camping and Caravan Park

Seaview, Keil Croft, Benderloch, Oban, Argyll, PA37 1QS Tel: 01631 720360
www.seaviewcaravanandcamping.co.uk

This site on a family croft has a view down Ardmucknish Bay to the island of Kerrera. Facilities include a shower block, a snack bar, and a room for campers with tables and a microwave oven. Most pitches have electricity. The sandy beach is a short walk away and forest walks are close by. An asphalt cycle route follows the general line of A828 for parts of the way between Connel and Fort William.

| NA 4 | NP 40 | 16 AMP | | |

Pub 2 miles. Shop 0.5 miles.

££££ CL CS WiFi

Directions: From Oban on A85 turn right onto A828 in Connel and cross Connel Bridge sp 'Fort William' (height limit 4.2m/13ft 6in). In 3 miles just past Benderloch village, turn left sp 'South Shian/Tralee'. The site is on the left in 0.25 miles.

GPS: N56°29.780' W005°24.648'
OS grid: 49 NM 901 387

April - October

North Ledaig Caravan Park 109

Connel, Oban, Argyll and Bute, PA37 1RU
Tel: 01631 710291
www.northledaigcaravanpark.co.uk

This immense park is situated alongside a 2 mile sand and shingle beach. Some of the pitches are almost at the water's edge and face the sea with panoramic views across to the beautiful Isle of Mull. Ardmucknish Bay is perfect for sailing and other water sports and provides safe bathing. The site is ideal for children, who can play on an adventure playground. About half the pitches are reserved for Caravan Club members. All pitches have electricity and everything is equipped and managed to the highest standard. Buses to Oban stop at the gate.

NA 30	NP 280	10 AMP		
WC					MG	MB

Pub 1 mile.

£££ 🐕 ♀♂ M CL CS (i) WiFi

Directions: From Oban on A85 turn right onto A828 in Connel and cross Connel Bridge sp 'Fort William' (height limit 4.2m/13ft 6in). After 1.5 miles, the site entrance is inconspicuously sp on the left.

GPS: N56°28.660' W005°23.935'
OS grid: 49 NM 907 368

Easter - October

Oban Caravan and Camping Park 110

Gallanachmore Farm, Gallanach Road, Oban, Argyll, PA34 4QH Tel: 01631 562425
www.obancaravanpark.com

This site is set alongside a coastal road with pitches in three areas overlooking the Sound of Kerrera. As the site is part of a working farm, it is divided into several areas on different levels and campers share territory with chickens and ducks. The staff are friendly and helpful and the site is well organised. There is a nearby diving school offering trials of the sport and bustling Oban has ferries and a range of excursions.

NA 25	NP 250	16 AMP		
WC					MG	MB

Pub and shops 2.5 miles. Slipway 0.5 miles.

£££ 🐕 ♀♂ M CL CS (i) WiFi

Directions: From Oban town centre follow sp 'Gallanach' and the campsite symbol past the ferry terminal and railway station. The site is 2.5 miles along the narrow coast road with passing places.

GPS: N56°23.395' W005°31.010'
OS grid: 49 NM 830 272

April - September

Fiunary Camping and Caravan Park and CS

Nr Lochaline, Morvern, Argyll, PA80 5XU
Tel: 01967 421225
www.campingandcaravanningclub.co.uk

This highly regarded site has many large, hedged pitches divided between two areas, some sloping gently down to the pebble beach beside the Sound of Mull. As a site open to the public, it accepts tents only. As a Camping and Caravanning Club CS, it can take up to 5 caravans or motorhomes, providing electricity for all of them. It is a peaceful, quiet place with innumerable birds and the chance to see otters and pine martens actually on the site's shore. The area has numerous forest walks, and hill walkers are well served.

| NA | 4 | NP | 10+5 | 6 AMP | | |

Pub, shop and slipway 5 miles at Lochaline.

£££ M CL CS WiFi

Directions: From Fort William, follow A82 south and then take the ferry to Corran. Follow A861 south for 12.5 miles and turn onto A884 just before Strontian sp 'Lochaline'. Follow A884 for 18 miles to Lochaline, then continue west on B849 sp 'Kirk Braie'. The site is in 4.5 miles on the left.

GPS: N56°33.117' W005°53.133'
OS grid: 49 NM 613 467

May - September

Killiechronan Campsite

Killiechronan Estate, Loch Na Keal,
Isle of Mull, PA72 6JU
Warden 07747 192443, estate 01680 300403

This is a quiet, away-from-it-all site situated on an elevated bank beside the rocky and grassy shore of Loch Na Keal across which the view extends. The ground is partly hard and partly soft. Minimal facilities at the estate buildings across the road are two toilets and a sink with hot and cold water. Horse riding is available nearby.

| NA | 1 | NP | 20 | 0 AMP | | |

Pub and shop 3.5 miles at Salen.

££££ M CL CS WiFi

Directions: From Craignure or Tobermory, travel to Salen. Then take B8035 southwest for 3 miles. Turn right onto B8073 and follow for 0.75 miles to the site by the shore. Register at estate buildings nearby.

GPS: N56°29.900' W006°00.233'
OS grid: 47 NM 537 412

All year

Fidden Farm Campsite

Fidden, Fionnphort, Isle of Mull, PA66 6BN
Tel: 01681 700427

The extensive pitching area on level, hard, well-drained, sandy turf gives wide views across the islet-strewn waters to the islands of Iona and Erraid. The sandy beach faces shallow water that is safe for swimming. A plain stone farm outbuilding belies the stylishly furnished washrooms. This remote, hospitable site is strongly recommended for visiting early or late in the season for the solitude and abundant wildlife while still having essential supplies in the nearby village. It is the nearest site to the ferry to Iona and cruises to Fingal's Cave in Staffa.

| NA 35 | NP 40 | 0 AMP | | |

| WC | ♿ | | | | | MG | MB |

Pub, shop and slipway at Fionnphort, 1.5 miles.

££££ 🐕 ♛♛ M CL CS ⓘ WiFi

Directions: From Craignure, take A849 for 37 miles to Fionnphort. Turn left in the village sp 'Fidden'. Farm and site in 1.5 miles.

GPS: N56°18.480' W006°21.830'
OS grid: 48 NM 302 214

April - October

Port Mor Centre Campsite

Port Charlotte, Isle of Islay, PA48 7UE
Tel: 01496 850441
www.islandofislay.co.uk/campsite.php

On an elevated bank above the rocky shore where otters may be seen, the sweeping view is across Loch Indaal to the southern part of the island. The 10 hard, level pitches with hook-ups for caravans and motorhomes stand on the bank near the beach, with tent pitches spread along the mown grass bank. Higher up towards the road are a playground, football pitch and the centre's magnificent building containing a café/restaurant, washrooms and full facilities, all immaculate for finish and cleanliness. In the locality are a museum and distilleries to visit. Buses pass the site. This community project warmly welcomes visitors.

| NA 6 | NP 55 | 16 AMP | | |

| WC | ♿ | | | | 🔲 | MG | MB |

Slipway 1.5 miles.

£££ 🐕 ♛♛ M CL CS ⓘ WiFi

Directions: The site is 0.5 miles south of Port Charlotte. Pass through the village and Port Mor Centre is on the left.

GPS: N55°44.006' W006°23.185'
OS grid: 60 NR 247 576

All year

Port Bàn Holiday Park

Kilberry, Tarbert, Argyll, PA29 6YD
Tel: 01880 770224
www.portban.com

Photo courtesy of Port Bàn Holiday Park

The commanding view from all areas is west to Islay and Jura, and south to Gigha. The small touring area is right beside the sandy beach and has a hook-up for each pitch. On the all-grass site, statics and seasonals are tiered steeply up to a cluster of buildings housing reception, a large games room with table tennis and billiards, a shop and a café with home baking. By the buildings is a tennis court, and a play castle is right by the shore. Port Bàn's appeal is its quiet, remote solitude. It is a welcoming, friendly little community.

| NA 12 | NP 6 | 16 AMP | | |

| WC | | | | | MG | MB |

Pub 1 mile.

£££ WiFi

Directions: From Tarbert, turn onto single-track A8024 sp 'Kilberry'. After approximately 14 miles, Port Bàn is sp on the right.

GPS: N55°49.783' W005°39.350'
OS grid: 62 NR 708 655

April - October

Point Sands Holiday Park

Tayinloan, Argyll, PA29 6XG
Tel: 01583 441263
www.pointsands.co.uk

Photo courtesy of Rebecca Maxwell Macdonald

This is a level site right on the sea where you can pitch directly next to the shore with absolutely superb views over the bay to the Isles of Gigha, Islay and Jura. The long sandy beach offers safe bathing, sailing, windsurfing and other water sports. The children's unfenced play area is in the camping field. This is the nearest site to the Gigha and Islay ferries. A safe, traffic-free pedestrian and cycle path is planned to give direct access to the Gigha ferry terminal. The Kintyre Way passes through the park.

| NA 16 | NP 60 | 16 AMP | | |

| WC | | | | | MG | MB |

Pub 1 mile. Showers 50p.

£££ WiFi

Directions: Take A83 for 17 miles from Tarbert towards Campbeltown. The site is on the seashore 1 mile down a clearly sp drive.

GPS: N55°40.319' W005°38.960'
OS grid: 62 NR 696 484

April - October

Muasdale Holiday Park

Muasdale, Tarbert, Argyll, PA29 6XD
Tel: 01583 421207
www.muasdaleholidays.com

Photo courtesy of Alison Clements

Since the the touring pitches are right beside the beach, you can jump from your pitch onto the soft white sand and will enjoy beautiful views of the islands. The site is split into two with statics on one side of the road and tourers and tents the other. Pitches are narrow and tents over 4m/12ft will require 2 pitches. This is an ideal location if you are looking for peace and tranquillity, and it is convenient for ferries to Arran, Gigha, Islay and Jura. There is a homely, heated toilet block.

| NA 2 | NP 10 | ☠ 10 AMP | | |

| WC | ♿ | 🚿 | | 🛁 | ⊙ | MG | MB |

Pub 4 miles. Shop in village 100m. Slipway at Tayinloan.

£££ 🐕 ♟ M CL CS ⓘ WiFi

Directions: Take A83 south from Tarbert and Muasdale is in 22.5 miles. The site is on the right with the house on the left.

GPS: N55°35.873' W005°41.148'
OS grid: 68 NR 678 399

Easter - October

Killegruer Caravan Site

Woodend, Glenbarr, Tarbert, Argyll,
PA29 6XB Tel: 01583 421241
www.killegruercaravansite.com

Photo courtesy of Anne Littleson

The site is mostly occupied with static caravans, but the 20 touring pitches of grass on firm sand are right next to the beach with a view across to the south of Islay. This is a nice, comfortable, tidy site isolated right on the west coast of the Kintyre Peninsula. The beach is sandy and interspersed with rocks, but body boarding should be possible. The site is within reasonable driving distance of Campbeltown.

| NA 4 | NP 30 | ☠ 16 AMP | | |

| WC | ♿ | 🚿 | | 🛁 | ⊙ | MG | MB |

Pub 1 mile. Shop 0.5 miles. Slipway 5 miles at Tayinloan.

££££ 🐕 ♟ M CL CS ⓘ WiFi

Directions: The site is clearly visible on the right 1 mile beyond Glenbarr village, 25.5 miles south of Tarbert on A83.

GPS: N55°33.363' W005°42.418'
OS grid: 68 NR 663 354

April - October

Machrihanish Camping and Caravan Park

East Trodigal, Machrihanish, Campbeltown, Argyll, PA28 6PT Tel: 01586 810366
www.campkintyre.co.uk

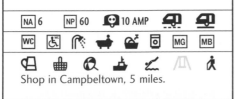

From this attractive site with widely spaced pitches on firm, well-kept grass, you can watch glorious sunsets over Islay and Jura. Some pitches have a view of the sea beyond the low dunes. Upgrading under new ownership has seen the addition of camping pods, a renewed electrical system and a colourful crazy golf course. The site has a small shop for essentials. Escape sea breezes by sitting in the garden by the burn. The Kintyre Way passes by. Buses run to Campbeltown.

| NA 6 | NP 60 | 10 AMP | | |

Shop in Campbeltown, 5 miles.

££££

Directions: Take A83 down the Kintyre Peninsula to Campbeltown. Follow B842, then B843 to the site on the outskirts of Machrihanish.

GPS: N55°25.383' W005°43.000'
OS grid: 68 NR 649 207

All year except November and February

Machribeg Campsite

Southend, Campbeltown, Argyll, PA28 6RW
Tel: 01586 830249

Although the site is right by the shore, pitches with a sea view are mostly occupied by seasonal caravans or statics, but in spring or autumn you may find a space from which you can look across to the Mull of Kintyre and Northern Ireland. Other pitches are lower lying and somewhat sheltered, though without the view. The long sandy beach is readily accessible. Several farm-type buildings house basic facilities and toilet emptying, showers being individually accessed by key available from the farm when registering. There are a few shops in Southend and many more in Campbeltown.

| NA 4 | NP 10 | 0 AMP | | |

Pub and shop 0.5 miles.

££££

Directions: Take A83 down the Kintyre Peninsula to Campbeltown, then B842 through Southend. At the end of the village, Machribeg farm drive is opposite the turning to the golf club. The site is clearly visible 0.25 miles further on.

GPS: N55°18.700' W005°39.200'
OS grid: 68 NR 684 080

April - September

Peninver Sands Caravan Park

Peninver, Campbeltown, Argyll, PA28 6QP
Tel: 01586 552262
www.peninver-sands.com

This community site makes a good night halt and lies between the shore and B842 along the scenic east coast of Kintyre. From the level, mown pitches, glimpses of Arran are obtained between the statics: stroll through the village for better views. Children have plenty of play space on grassy areas both within and outside the site fence, also on the beach of pebbles and some sand.

| NA 2 | NP 10 | | | |

££££ 🐕 †† M CL CS ⓘ WiFi

Directions: Take A83 down the Kintyre Peninsula to Campbeltown. Turn north onto B842 for 4.5 miles to Peninver. The touring site is in the middle of the village. Reception is in the statics park at the south end of the village at the foot of a steep hill.

Scottish
TOURIST BOARD
★★★★
SMALL
HOLIDAY
PARK

GPS: N55°28.016' W005°32.783'
OS grid: 68 NR 761 251

March - October

Carradale Bay Caravan Park

Carradale, Campbeltown, Argyll, PA28 6QG
Tel: 01583 431665
www.carradalebay.com

The park is alongside a 1 mile long, south-facing sandy beach backed by dunes. Landscaping provides small camping areas protected by shrubs and bushes, each pitch having good sea views across to the Isle of Arran. The motorhome length limit is 8.6m/28ft. Situated in an area of outstanding natural beauty, this site is suitable for families as there is plenty of walking and cycling in the adjacent Forestry Commission land.

| NA 12 | NP 75 | 10/16 AMP | | |

Pub 15 mins. Shop 1 mile. Internet connection available in reception area.

££££ 🐕 †† M CL CS ⓘ WiFi

Directions: The site is located off B842, halfway between Claonaig and Campbeltown. Turn off B842 onto B879 sp 'Carradale' with the campsite symbol. Follow the single-track road 0.5 miles to the sea. The site entrance is clearly sp. Users of large units should approach from Campbeltown.

GPS: N55°34.850' W005°29.150'
OS grid: 69 NR 804 374

Easter - September

Argyll Caravan Park

Inveraray, Argyll, PA32 8XT
Tel: 01499 302285
www.argyllcaravanpark.com

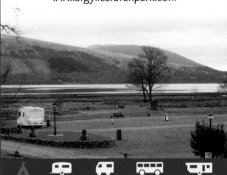

The touring area beside a small river has a view out over Loch Fyne and is one of the smartest and most conveniently laid out to be found, with many pull-through pitches. It is separated from a large, terraced area of quality park homes with gardens. In the reception area is a substantial shop, restaurant, bar, laundry and hair salon. The waters of the loch are popular for boating, fishing and diving, with a slipway and boat park on the site. Outstanding local attractions are Crarae Garden, Auchindrain Open-Air Museum, and Inveraray Castle and historic jail.

| NA 30 | NP 45 | 16 AMP | | |

Slipway on site.

£££**£**

Directions: The site is 2 miles south of Inveraray adjacent to A83. The site entrance is clearly sp with the campsite symbol and statics are visible from the road.

GPS: N56°12.183' W005°06.450'
OS grid: 56 NN 073 055

April or Easter - October

Ardgartan

Ardgartan, Arrochar, Dunbartonshire,
G83 7AR Tel: 01301 702293
www.forestholidays.co.uk

This Forest Holidays site lies on a promontory extending into Loch Long and within the Argyll Forest Park. Campers are no longer accepted, but their extensive range of cabins will cater for every type of holiday from romantic getaways to active family breaks. The view takes in Arrochar at the head of the loch, cradled by the 'Arrochar Alps'. The site's shop, café, bar and terrace will keep you watered and fed for days. From the Forest Centre, 0.5 miles away, a network of footpaths and mountain bike routes radiates.

| NA 11 | NP 100 | 16 AMP | | |

Pub and shop 1.5 miles.

£££**£**

Directions: From Glasgow, follow A82 beside Loch Lomond to Tarbet. Take A83 towards Inveraray and continue 2.5 miles beyond the junction with A814. The site is on the left as the road swings away from the lochside sp 'Ardgartan'.

GPS: N56°11.383' W004°46.917'
OS grid: 56 NN 275 030

All year

Ardlui CL 125

Ardlui, Kings Cross, Brodick, Isle of Arran,
KA27 8RB Tel: 01770 700557
www.5vandirectory.co.uk/Ardlui_CL.html

From its high vantage point, part of the *CL* field has a panoramic view over Brodick Bay and Holy Island. Some firm, level spots can be found, but elsewhere the ground slopes and is very soft when wet. A long mains lead may be needed to reach one of the sockets. A well-maintained outhouse provides a shower, toilet, washing machine and dryer. The nearest beach is 2 miles away at Whiting Bay or Lamlash.

| NA 3 | NP 5 | 16 AMP | | |

Pub, shop, beach and slipway 2 miles.

££££ 🐕 ♯♯ M *CL* CS ⓘ WiFi

Directions: From Brodick, take A841 to Lamlash. From the next hairpin bend, continue for 2 miles and turn left sp 'Ardlui' onto a farm track. At 2 *CL* signs, fork left into Ardlui *CL*.

GPS: N55°30.633' W005°06.033'
OS grid: 69 NS 045 285

All year

Seal Shore
Camping and Touring Site 126

Kildonan, Isle of Arran, KA27 8SE
Tel: 01770 820320
www.campingarran.com

The slight, south-facing slope gives all pitches a panoramic view taking in Pladda Island close by and Ailsa Craig beyond. In the distance are Southend in Argyll and the Ayrshire coast. Otters frequent the mainly rocky shore by the site, as well as seals and sea birds. The adjacent Kildonan Hotel provides meals, stores and papers. Buses and the Arran Coast Path pass by. The owner sometimes has freshly caught mackerel to give to campers. The adjacent Kildonan Hotel has a bar/restaurant and the on site shop stocks essentials. There is electricity for 16 pitches, of which 8 are hard.

| NA 3 | NP 53 | 16 AMP | | |

£££ 🐕 ♯♯ M *CL* CS ⓘ WiFi

Directions: The site is off A841 on the southeastern coast of the Isle of Arran, 3.5 miles south of Whiting Bay. Turn off A841 sp 'Seal Shore Camping 1.1 miles'. The site is at the bottom of the hill on the left.

GPS: N55°26.467' W005°06.850'
OS grid: 69 NS 032 207

April - October

Craig Tara Holiday Park

Dunure Road, Ayr, Ayrshire, KA7 4LB
Tel: 01292 265141
www.haven.com

The touring area is at the top of this very large holiday park that slopes right down to a beach of sand and shingle. From the first 12 pitches, Arran in the distance and the lower Clyde Estuary can just be seen. All pitches are hard and level and have electricity, with 17 fully serviced. The park has its own golf course, restaurants, supermarket, and separate entertainment areas for adults and children. There is also an indoor centre offering archery, fencing and a climbing wall. A frequent bus service runs to Ayr. Nearby are the new Robert Burns Visitor Centre and a popular animal park.

| NA 2.5 | NP 44 | 16 AMP | | |

Slipway 3 miles.

££££ 🐕 †† M CL CS (i) WiFi
Including passes

Directions: From the centre of Ayr, take A719 south sp 'Dunure' for 3.5 miles to the site on the right. Touring reception and the pitches are on the right immediately after turning off the road.

GPS: N55°25.555' W004°41.137'
OS grid: 70 NS 303 185

March - October

Culzean Castle Camping and Caravanning Club Site

Culzean, Maybole, Ayrshire, KA19 8JX
Tel: 01655 760627
www.campingandcaravanningclub.co.uk

The site is in the grounds of the magnificent Culzean Castle with good views across arable fields to the sea, particularly from the front row of pitches. In wet weather the ground is very soft and motorhomes are restricted to the 19 hardstandings. The mountains of the Isle of Arran litter the horizon, creating spectacular sunsets. The sea is about a 2.5-mile drive away. A range of events are held at Culzean Castle, which is open to the public and free to National Trust members.

| NA 5 | NP 90 | 10 AMP | | |

Pub and shop 4 miles. Slipway 2.5 miles.

£££ 🐕 †† M CL CS (i) WiFi

Directions: The site is adjacent to A719 halfway between Maybole and Maidens. Turn off A719 into the entrance of Culzean Castle and Country Park, also sp with the campsite symbol. In 50m turn right into the site.

GPS: N55°21.173' W004°46.165'
OS grid: 70 NS 247 102

March - October

Balkenna Caravan Site

Girvan Road, Turnberry, Ayrshire,
KA26 9LN
Tel: 01655 331692

From this little, level, all-grass site beside the coast road, the view is across one field and the stony shore directly out to Ailsa Craig in the southern approaches to the Firth of Clyde. The modest toilets and showers are modern and very clean. Beside the site and forming part of the same establishment is a café run by the owner and serving meals cooked to order and refreshments all day. Whether you are passing by or stopping for the night, this place is welcoming.

NA 0.25 | NP 15 | 16 AMP

WC

Slipway 1.5 miles. Pub 2 miles. Shop 4 miles.

£££ M CL CS WiFi

Directions: The site is 0.5 miles south of Turnberry on A77, near Balkenna Tearooms.

GPS: N55°18.087' W004°50.067'
OS grid: 76 NS 203 045

April - October

Wig Bay Holiday Park

Kirkcolm, Loch Ryan, Stranraer, DG9 0PS
Tel: 01776 853233
www.wigbayholidaypark.com

In this large, neatly kept statics site, well sheltered from the west, the touring area has a privileged position close to the water. Level at the rear and sloping gradually towards the sea at the front, it gives all a view across Loch Ryan to the ferry terminals of Cairnryan. Adjacent to the touring area is a small, heated indoor pool. Water sports are well provided for locally. Gannets can be watched plunge diving just off the shore: fishermen make catches, too, but from the stony beach.

NA 0.5 | NP 18 | 16 AMP

WC MG

Slipway 0.5 miles. Pub 1.5 miles. Shop 2 miles.

£££ M CL CS WiFi

Directions: The site is 4.25 miles northwest of Stranraer adjacent to A718. The entrance is on the left and is clearly sp.

GPS: N54°56.790' W005°04.235'
OS grid: 82 NX 033 657

March - October

Castle Bay Holiday Park

Portpatrick, Stranraer, Dumfries and Galloway,
DG9 9AA Tel: 01776 810462
www.castlebayholidaypark.co.uk

The winding site road threads among neat statics with some attractive gardens to the elevated, mainly level touring area with views extending to Ireland in clear conditions. A hard surface with the best views holds 12 unmarked pitches. Of the remainder on grass, some are level and most have electricity. The gaunt remains of Dunskey Castle are a feature on the clifftop. Site facilities include a games room, and the shop has basic provisions.

| NA 2 | NP 45 | 6/10 AMP | | |

| WC | | | | | | MG | MB |

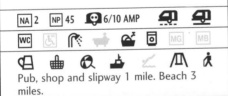

Pub, shop and slipway 1 mile. Beach 3 miles.

£££ | M | CL | CS | (i) | WiFi

Directions: From Stranraer, take A77 to Portpatrick. Take the 1st left-hand turn past the war memorial. Continue for 0.75 miles, going under an old railway bridge. After a further 50 yards, the site entrance is on the right.

Scottish TOURIST BOARD ★★ SMALL HOLIDAY PARK

GPS: N54°50.313' W005°06.078'
OS grid: 82 NX 007 534

March - October

South Port O'Spittal *CL*

Portpatrick, Stranraer, Wigtownshire,
DG9 9AQ Tel: 07808 860393
www.portpatrickholidaypark.co.uk

Passing across the sea vista are ferries running between Loch Ryan and Northern Ireland, which can be seen in some detail on clear days. Pitches comprise 4 slightly sloping hardstandings, each in its own bay between grassy banks. The 4 level grass pitches have the better view past fields where belted Galloway cattle graze. The *CL* is painstakingly laid out and cared for and provides separate small units for ladies, for gents, and for laundry and dishwashing. At much visited Portpatrick nearby, the lifeboat is central in the community.

| NA 0.75 | NP 5 | 16 AMP | | |

| WC | | | | | | MG | MB |

Beach 1 mile and others 3 miles.

££££ | M | *CL* | CS | (i) | WiFi

Directions: From Portpatrick, take A77 northeast for 2 miles. Fork right onto B7042 and follow for 1 mile. Fork right again, sp 'Meoul', and follow road for 1.25 miles. At the 3-way junction, take a track almost straight ahead to Port O'Spittal and the *CL*, sp with a Caravan Club sign.

GPS: N54°49.593' W005°03.660'
OS grid: 82 NX 032 519

March - November

New England Bay Caravan Club Site

Port Logan, Drummore, Dumfries and
Galloway, DG9 9NX Tel: 01776 860275
www.caravanclub.co.uk

The mostly level, mostly grass pitches of this
delightful site are dispersed over a large area
and on two levels. Many have a fine view
across much of Luce Bay. The long stretch of
sandy beach is ideal for swimming, fishing
and launching dinghies or kayaks. Boat
fishing in the bay is popular, and the site has
a boat-washing facility. So large and widely
spaced are some of the pitches that various
games can be played there without
inconveniencing the neighbours. In wet
weather, the games room comes into its own.
Logan Botanic Garden and attractive Port
Logan are nearby.

NA 17	NP 159	16 AMP		
WC	WC			MG	MB

Slipway 3 miles. Pub and shop 4 miles.

£££

Directions: The site is adjacent to A716 on
the eastern coast of the Rhins of Galloway
peninsula, halfway between Sandhead and
Kirkmaiden. At the junction of B7065 and
A716, keep left to stay on A716 and follow
for 1.25 miles. The site is sp on the left.

GPS: N54°44.275' W004°55.285'
OS grid: 82 NX 121 422

March - November

Ardwell Caravan Park

Killaser, Ardwell, Wigtownshire, DG9 9LS
Tel: 01776 860294

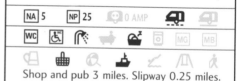

This is a very pleasant, simple, level site with
superb views across the whole of Luce Bay as
far round as Burrow Head and down into the
Irish Sea. Pitches are close to the stony
shore where some sand appears at low tide.
It is as peaceful as you could ask for. Within
a traditional stone building, facilities with
modern equipment are smartly decorated
and include a comprehensively fitted
disabled room. Immediately across the road
is Ardwell Gardens with woodland walking
and a walled garden.

NA 5	NP 25	0 AMP		
WC	WC			MG	MB

Shop and pub 3 miles. Slipway 0.25 miles.

£££

Directions: The site is adjacent to A716 on
the eastern coast of the Rhins of Galloway
peninsula, 3 miles south of Sandhead. The
site is on the left on entering Ardwell, sp
'Ardwell Caravan Site' on the gable end of
the white house at the site entrance.

GPS: N54°46.245' W004°56.453'
OS grid: 82 NX 110 456

April - September

Sands of Luce Holiday Park

Sandhead, Stranraer, Dumfries and Galloway,
DG9 9JN Tel: 01766 830456
www.sandsofluceholidaypark.co.uk

One touring area has an unobstructed view over all of Luce Bay. A second touring area is encircled by sheltering trees. Pitches are all level with electricity. The site has direct access to the long sandy beach. The newly established Mull of Galloway Trail from Stranraer to the Mull passes through the site. In the vicinity are six fine gardens for visiting.

| NA 5 | NP 25 | 16 AMP | | |

Shop 0.25 miles.

££££ 🐕 ♂♀ M CL CS ⓘ WiFi

Directions: The site is adjacent to A716 on the eastern coast of the Rhins of Galloway peninsula, 0.5 miles north of Sandhead. The site is clearly sp on both sides of the road.

GPS: N54°48.935' W004°57.610'
OS grid: 82 NX 102 507

March - October

Kings Green Caravan Site

South Street, Port William, Newton Stewart,
Wigtownshire, DG8 9SH Tel: 01988 700489
www.kingsgreencaravanpark.com

This hospitable, well-rated, community-owned site lies right beside the stony shore, giving a panorama across Luce Bay to the Rhins of Galloway and the aptly named Scares Rocks. Of the level grass pitches, 33 have electricity. The immaculately cleaned, modern facilities are the pride of the management committee. Crafts and essential supplies can be found in the village, whose picturesque harbour was the commercial heart of Port William in bygone times. The smuggling of those days has presumably declined, too!

| NA 2 | NP 30 | 16 AMP | | |

££££ 🐕 ♂♀ M CL CS ⓘ WiFi

Directions: The site is on the right adjacent to A747 at the far end of Port William village, 13 miles south of Glenluce.

GPS: N54°45.373' W004°34.916'
OS grid: 82 NX 340 430

April - October

Knock School Caravan Park

Monreith, Newton Stewart, Wigtownshire, DG8 8NJ Tel: 01988 700414
www.knockschool.co.uk

This beautiful little site, situated in the grounds of a former local school, is lovingly tended by its owners. The distant view of the Solway Firth may be extremely limited, but walk 0.5 miles to Monreith Bay for a vista of coastal scenery, a shoreside golf course and Monreith village. The site provides good shelter for the 11 caravan pitches on luxuriant grass. There is a little level hardstanding for motorhomes in times of need and 4 pitches for tents are in a smaller enclosure.

| NA 1 | NP 15 | 10 AMP | | |

| WC | | | | | | MG | MB |

Beach 0.5 miles. Pub, shop and slipway 3 miles.

££££ M CL CS WiFi

Directions: The site is 3 miles south of Port William on A747, sp on the side of the house.

GPS: N54°43.988' W004°32.142'
OS grid: 83 NX 369 405

Easter - September

Burrowhead Holiday Village

Isle of Whithorn, Newton Stewart, Dumfries and Galloway, DG8 8JB Tel: 01988 500252
www.burrowheadholidayvillage.co.uk

Photo courtesy of Breathing Space Productions

The Isle of Man, a mere 18 miles away, figures prominently in the wide sea view from this extensive clifftop site. The Lake District hills may also be seen. Caravan pitches are scattered informally across two undulating touring areas. Tents occupy a level, well-sheltered area in a hollow. A play area, crazy golf, a heated pool, and pitch and putt provide outdoor activity. 1 large building houses entertainment accommodation, restaurant and shop. The spectacular cliffs now suited to birdwatching and rock fishing were used in the Second World War for testing anti-aircraft weapons: remnants can be seen.

| NA 10 | NP 112 | 16 AMP | | |

| WC | | | | | | MG | MB |

Slipway 2 miles. Sandy beach 6 miles.

££££ M CL CS WiFi

Directions: From the Isle of Whithorn, follow sp 'Burrowhead' southwest along a very minor road for 2 miles to the site.

GPS: N54°41.125' W004°24.451'
OS grid: 83 NX 451 345

March - October

Garlieston Caravan Club Site

Garlieston, Newton Stewart, Dumfries and
Galloway, DG8 8BS Tel: 01988 600636
www.caravanclub.co.uk

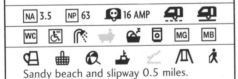

The main part of this level, members-only
site is right on the waterfront between the
village and a busy little harbour. All pitches,
mostly hard, look out over shallow Garlieston
Bay and have views along the village
waterfront and past the pier out into
Wigtown Bay. A river divides this area in two,
but they are linked by a vehicle bridge. The
second part is lawned, gardened, and
sheltered by woods. Woodland paths in
Galloway House estate lead to Rigg Bay
which is famed as a proving ground for parts
of the mobile Mulberry Harbour used in the
Second World War.

| NA | 3.5 | NP | 63 | 16 AMP | | |

| WC | | | | | | MG | MB |

Sandy beach and slipway 0.5 miles.

£££ ♞ ♦♦ M CL CS ⓘ WiFi

Directions: From Wigtown, follow A714,
then A746, then B7004 for 8 miles to
Garlieston. At a sharp right turn, turn left to
the waterfront, then right to the site.

GPS: N54°47.262' W004°22.105'
OS grid: 83 NX 478 462

March - November

Mossyard Caravan Park

Gatehouse of Fleet, Castle Douglas,
Dumfries and Galloway, DG7 2ET
Tel: 01557 840226 www.mossyard.co.uk

This is a mostly level, nicely mown site with
sea views from most pitches. Indeed, some
pitches lie very close to the rocky and sandy
shore. The site is part of the working farm of
the McConchie family, who have welcomed
campers for four generations. Thanks to its
wide open, grassy areas, this beautiful and
exceptionally well-maintained site offers
visitors a great feeling of space. The sandy
beach is ideal for launching dinghies and
kayaks. The surrounding landscape of farms,
woodland and coast is treasured for a host of
countryside activities, a wide range of which
is provided by nearby Laggan Outdoor.

| NA | 6.5 | NP | 36 | 16 AMP | | |

| WC | | | | | | MG | MB |

Pub and shop 1 mile. Showers 20p.

££££ ♞ ♦♦ M CL CS ⓘ WiFi

Directions: The site is off A75 halfway
between Newton Stewart and Castle
Douglas. Coming from Dumfries, turn left
3.25 miles beyond the Water of Fleet bridge,
by the conspicuous sp 'Mossyard'.

GPS: N54°50.433' W004°15.625'
OS grid: 83 NX 549 516

March - October

Auchenlarie Holiday Park

141

Gatehouse of Fleet, Castle Douglas, Dumfries and Galloway, DG7 2EX Tel: 01556 506200
www.swalwellholidaygroup.co.uk

This is a very large, beautifully maintained holiday park with extensive, excellent facilities making it a high quality, all-singing and all-dancing holiday destination. The main touring area is high up, giving sweeping sea views across Wigtown Bay to the Isle of Whithorn. Looming above the far horizon, ghostlike, is the Isle of Man. The caravan pitches are on asphalt or gravel and almost all are level. There are also some Super pitches. The tent areas do not share much of the view. The site has its own sandy, sheltered cove reached by a wide, gently sloping gravel cliff path.

| NA | 8 | NP | 70 | ☠ 16 AMP | | |

| WC | ♿ | 🚿 | 🛁 | 🧺 | ▣ | MG | MB |

Shop at Sandhead. Slipway 0.5 miles.

£££ 🐕 ♟ M CL CS ⓘ WiFi

Directions: The site is adjacent to A75 between Newton Stewart and Castle Douglas, 4.25 miles southwest of the Water of Fleet bridge.

GPS: N54°50.629' W004°16.814'
OS grid: 83 NX 536 522

March - October

Seaward Caravan Park

142

Dhoon Bay, Kirkcudbright, Dumfries and Galloway, DG6 4TJ Tel: 01557 331079
www.gillespie-leisure.co.uk

From the two rows of level, hard pitches with electricity, the view between trees is across to St Mary's Isle and down Kirkcudbright Bay to the Solway Firth. The view is more open now than our photo from 2012 shows. The level tent area is well sheltered by hedges all around, so without the view. Across the road, the shore is rocky, but low tide reveals a big expanse of sand. The site has its own screened, heated outdoor pool. In addition to the tastefully modernised facilities, other features are a TV lounge, games room, book exchange, pitch and putt, and a shop for basic provisions.

| NA | 3 | NP | 36 | ☠ 16 AMP | | |

| WC | ♿ | 🚿 | 🛁 | 🧺 | ▣ | MG | MB |

Slipway 1 mile. Pub 3 miles.

£££ 🐕 ♟ M CL CS ⓘ WiFi

Directions: From Kirkcudbright, take A755 across the river. In 0.5 miles, turn left onto B727 sp 'Borgue' and follow for 1.75 miles to the site on the right. Entry requires a sharp turn but with adequate space, then a short climb up the drive.

GPS: N54°49.142' W004°04.968'
OS grid: NX 662 491

March - October

Solway View Campsite CS

Balmangan Farm, Borgue, Kirkcudbright,
Dumfries and Galloway, DG6 4TR
Tel: 01557 870206 www.solwayviewholidays.com

Across the farm's fields, the outlook is to the peaceful waters of Kirkcudbright Bay. This view is shared by the 5 caravan pitches on the upper part, several wigwams and 25 tent pitches further down. All the caravan pitches have electricity and are hardstanding and 10 tent pitches have a hook-up. All pitches are level. The site is run in an environmentally conscious way: clothes drying, for example, is done in a specially designed open tent. Despite its capacity, the site is still a CS under original regulations. The area around Borgue is rich in history, and Kirkcudbright is renowned as an artists' town.

| NA | 2.5 | NP | 30 | ☠ 16 AMP | | |

Beach 0.5 miles. Pub, shop and slipway 2 miles.

£££ 🐕 †† M CL CS ⓘ WiFi

Directions: From Kirkcudbright, take A755 across the river. In 0.5 miles, turn left onto B727 sp 'Borgue' and follow for 3.25 miles. Turn left sp 'Ross Bay' and 'Brighouse Bay'. After 0.75 miles, fork left sp 'Solway View'. Reception is in 0.75 miles at the farmhouse on the right. The site is 200m beyond the farmhouse on the left.

GPS: N54°47.190' W004°05.898'
OS grid: NX 652 455

All year

Castle Point Caravan Site

Rockcliffe, by Dalbeattie, Dumfries and
Galloway, DG5 4QL Tel: 01556 630248
www.castlepointcc.com

Sea, island and mountain views are enjoyed from the site, which is very well maintained, clean and tidy. Facilities include a secure bike store and a wet room. A fairly steep and rough path takes you to a small cove near Castle Point. The 10-mins walk to the point has exciting views of the sea, and there are good walks in the area, including marked paths to Sandyhills and Kipford. Rockcliffe has a safe and interesting beach, about 1 mile away.

| NA | 3 | NP | 15 | ☠ 16 AMP | | |

Pub 0.5 miles. Shop 1 mile.

£££ 🐕 †† M CL CS ⓘ WiFi

Directions: From Dalbeattie, take A710 southwards. After 5 miles, turn right sp 'Rockcliffe'. At the brow of the hill on entering Rockcliffe, turn left sp 'Castle Point Caravan Site'. Drive down to the end of Barcloy Road and straight ahead up a private farm road to the site.

GPS: N54°51.565' W003°47.065'
OS grid: 84 NX 855 532

Easter - October

Sandyhills Bay Leisure Park

Sandyhills, Dalbeattie, Dumfries and Galloway, DG5 4NY Tel: 01387 780257
www.gillespie-leisure.co.uk

This is a really attractive site that is professionally maintained. It is ideal for families and has a useful shop and good facilities. The long sandy beach is directly accessible from the site and has a good tidal range, and even some salt marsh. The bay provides safe swimming and the wooded hill provides a harmonious backdrop to the site. The area is dotted with smugglers' coves that are accessible at low tide.

| NA 4 | NP 54 | ☠ 16 AMP | | |

Pub and shop 5 mins.

£££ £

Directions: Take the A710 coast road from Dalbeattie sp 'Solway Coast'. The site is on the right at Sandyhills village just past the golf course.

GPS: N54°52.795' W003°43.852'
OS grid: 84 NX 890 549

April - October

John Paul Jones Birthplace Museum *CL*

Arbigland Estate, Kirkbean, Dumfries, Kirkcudbrightshire, DG2 8BQ
Tel: 01387 880613 www.jpj.demon.co.uk

The whole area of the *CL* is hard surfaced and well sheltered among trees, with a low rose hedge between it and fields. Beyond the fields is a wide, distant panorama of the Solway Firth and the Lake District hills. The view may be restricted as the hedge grows during the season. A circular walk from the *CL* follows the fossil-rich shore, farmland, and woods. Several nature reserves are in the vicinity. The museum tells the story of the controversial naval adventurer.

| NA 0.25 | NP 5 | ☠ 0 AMP | | |

Beach 0.75 miles. Pub 2 miles. Shop 3 miles.

££££

Directions: Take A710 to Kirkbean. Turn off A710 sp 'Carsethorn'. Turn right in 200m sp 'John Paul Jones Cottage'. Follow road for 1.25 miles to end. Turn left, and then right at the main gates. The site is sp on the left in 0.25 miles. Reception is at the museum. The approach is potholed and may be overgrown.

GPS: N54°53.922' W003°34.845'
OS grid: NX 987 571

April - October

Moss-side Farm *CL* 147

Cummertrees, Annan, Dumfriesshire,
DG12 5PU Tel: 01461 700220
www.caravanclub.co.uk

The wide, well-drained, level, hard pitches
have a view across a field to the vast expanse
of the Solway Firth alternating between sea
and miles of sand flats. Beyond are the hills
of the Lake District. An asphalt lane leads to
the shore, which is a fine vantage point for
birdwatchers and has scope for dog walkers.
A homely facilities area has been built into a
corner of a barn that also has eggs for sale,
a library, and abundant local information.
The owner calls to meet her visitors.

| NA 1 | NP 5 | 12 AMP | | |

| WC | | | | | MG | MB |

Pub and campsite shop 1 mile. Other
shops 5 miles.

££££ M CL CS WiFi

Directions: From Annan, take B724 west to
Cummertrees. Turn left opposite a red phone
box along an unmarked narrow lane for 0.75
miles. At the *CL* sign, turn left to the site
beyond a large barn. There is no access from
Powfoot.

GPS: N54°58.628' W003°21.526'
OS grid: NY 133 653

All year

Queensberry Bay Holiday Park 148

Powfoot, Annan, Dumfriesshire, DG12 5PN
Tel: 01461 700205
www.queensberrybay.co.uk

This large site, mainly for statics and
seasonal caravans, has two areas for tourers,
both with electricity. 10 level pitches right on
the shore of the Solway Firth give sweeping
views across the estuary to the Cumbrian
Fells. 20 more almost level pitches occupy a
field away from the water. Tents use an
adjoining field. Sumptuous facilities are in
rooms each containing shower, basin, and
WC. Tenters are well provided for with a
kitchen cum dining room. A spa pool, sauna,
and hot tub complex can be rented, and a
range of massage treatments is offered.

| NA 17 | NP 30 | 10 AMP | | |

| WC | | | | | MG | MB |

££££ M CL CS WiFi

Directions: From Annan, take B724 west for
2.25 miles. Turn left by a brightly painted
bus shelter sp 'Powfoot' and 'Queensberry
Bay'. Continue 1.25 miles through the village
and along the seafront to the site.

GPS: N54°58.483' W003°20.847'
OS grid: 85 NY 132 653

February - November

INDEX

INDEX

Vicarious Shop

- Driving tour suitable for Motorbikes, Cars, Campervans and Motorhomes
- Details car parking, campsites, motorhome stopovers and hotels
- GPS coordinates provided for all sights and accommodation
- Town plans and walking tours for easy navigation on foot

Road Trip Europe
The Great War and More

Bastogne, Battle of the Bulge,

Brugge, Belgian Beer.

Battlefields of World War I.

Big National parks, Bashful wild cats.

Beautiful Mosel Valley, Bouquet of Wine.

Valkenburg Bountiful Christmas Markets.

A DRIVING TOUR

This driving tour encompasses five cities, four countries, and two world wars. The tour visits one of the most beautiful sections of river in Europe, a Roman capital, a national park where wild cats roam free and a town where Christmas decorations are sold all year. It will take you from the highest point in the Netherlands to below the streets of Arras.

To order, give us a call or visit our website to buy online.

Vicarious Shop

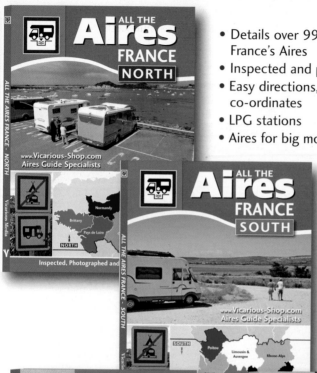

- Details over 99 per cent of France's Aires
- Inspected and photographed Aires
- Easy directions, On-site GPS co-ordinates
- LPG stations
- Aires for big motorhomes

Motorhomes have the privilege of staying on Motorhome Stopovers, known as Aires.

To order, give us a call or visit our website to buy online.

0131 208 3333   www.Vicarious-Shop.com

CAMPSITE SUBMISSION FORM

Please use this form to update the site information in this guide. We particularly need good photographs that represent the site and where possible show the sea view. Nominations for new sites are very welcome. If a site is already listed, complete only sections where changes apply. Please fill in answers in capital letters and circle appropriate symbols.

Site Name:

Address:

Postcode:

Tel. No:

Website:

Units accepted by campsite *Please circle 1 or more symbols as appropriate*

▲ Tent   🚐 Touring caravan   🚐 Motorhome

🚌 Large vehicles   🚐 Holiday accommodation for hire

Description of site:

NA Number of acres: NP Number of pitches:

⚡ Electricity available and amperage:

Symbols, facilities *Please circle as appropriate*

🚐 Level pitches   🚐 All season/hard standing pitches   WC Toilets   ♿ Disabled toilets

🚿 Showers   🛁 Family bathroom/shower room   Laundry   Dishwashing facilities

MG Motorhome wastewater disposal   MB Motorhome toilet waste disposal

Symbols, amenities *Please circle as appropriate*

Pub/bar   Shop   Beach   Slipway

Children's play area   Footpath   Swimming pool indoor or outdoor

Please see overleaf

CAMPSITE SUBMISSION FORM

Please circle as appropriate

Cost based on two people, one caravan or motorhome with electric in August. Guide prices only.

£   Up to £10 per night   **££**   £10-17 per night

£££ £17-35 per night   **££££** £35 or more per night

🐕 Dogs allowed onsite   👥 Adults (Over 18) only   **Ⓜ**   Members only

CS   Certified Site   CL   Certified Location

ⓘ   Internet available   WiFi   WiFi Available

Directions to site:

....

....

....

Awards: Scottish Tourist Board

OS grid references – 1:50,000

GPS Coordinates in the following format: N49°14.988' W000°16.838'

Opening and closing dates:

Photo(s) included: ☐ None   ☐ Emailed   ☐ Photo(s) posted with form

email pictures to: gomotorhoming@hotmail.co.uk

Name and email or address - so information can be credited:

Please use a separate form for each campsite. Send completed forms to:
Vicarious books, 62 Tontine Street, Folkestone, Kent, CT20 1JP
ask@vicariousbooks.co.uk

Thank you very much for your time.

By supplying details and photographs you are giving unrestricted publication and reproduction rights to Vicarious Books Ltd.